MAPPING

the

TERRITORY

MAPPING

the

TERRITORY

SELECTED NONFICTION

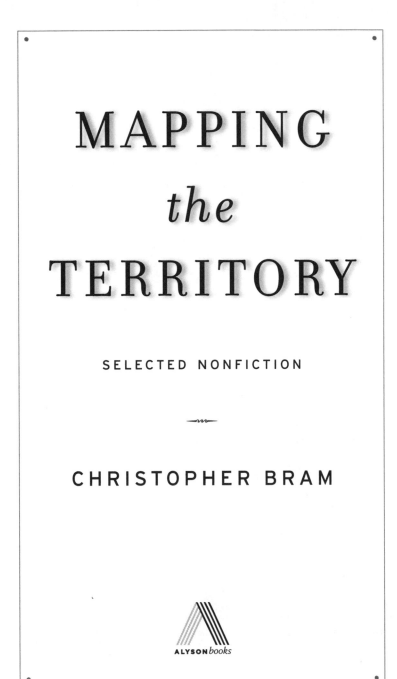

CHRISTOPHER BRAM

ALYSON*books*

Mapping the Territory

Published by Alyson Books
245 West 17th Street, Suite 1200, New York, NY 10011
www.alyson.com

ALYSON*books*

10 9 8 7 6 5 4 3 2 1

ISBN-10: 1-59350-143-9
ISBN-13: 978-1-59350-143-3

Library of Congress Cataloging-in-Publication data is on file.

Cover design by Lorie Pagnozzi
Book interior by Maria E. Torres, Neuwirth & Associates, Inc.

Printed in the United States of America
Distributed by Consortium Book Sales and Distribution
Distribution in the United Kingdom by Turnaround Publisher Services Ltd

To
Patrick Merla

CONTENTS

—◇—

MAPPING

the

TERRITORY

INTRODUCTION

—⁓—

I AM A NOVELIST who sometimes writes
essays and book reviews. It's the sort of
occasional prose usually described as done
with the left hand, only I'm left-handed so
the phrase doesn't work for me. I've been
producing these nonfiction pieces for thirty
years now. They are more literally personal
than my novels and I like to think they form
an accidental autobiography, one of ideas
and opinions as well as events. I have written about coming out in Virginia and about
sitting on my stoop in New York City, but I've

also written about Henry James, children's books, horror movies, straight male fiction, and gay marriage.

Here are my favorite pieces, arranged in a kind of chronological order so that they might suggest a life story if you read the book from beginning to end. You are free, of course, just to skip around. I have resisted the temptation to add postscripts and updates other than those written at the time of first publication.

I've been fortunate in the editors who asked for my work over the years. Patrick Merla invited me to write book reviews for *Christopher Street* magazine back in 1978, shortly after he published my first gay short story there. He was followed by Tom Steele. The late John Preston asked me to contribute to his nonfiction anthologies about gay life, *Hometowns* and *Friends and Lovers*, and Jim Marks frequently requested reviews for *Lambda Book Report*. The photographer Robert Giard invited me to write an essay about gay male literature for *Particular Voices*, his book of author photos, which is how "Mapping the Territory" came about; Joan Nestle wrote the essay about lesbian literature. (Giard too is now sadly gone.) Larry Mass asked for a contribution to his collection of essays about Larry Kramer. (This led to the inevitable second thoughts about Kramer, which I delivered at a public reading; they are printed here for the first time.) Ian Britain published an early version of my Henry James essay in *Meanjin*, the arts quarterly in Australia. Things came around full circle when I began to work with Patrick Merla again, first when I wrote "Slow Learners" for his collection of coming-out stories, *Boys Like Us*, and then, when he was editor of the *James White*

Review, with three long essays: "Can Straight Men Still Write?," "A Body in Books," and "A Queer Monster."

I often joke that Patrick made me a gay writer when he first published my short story—if I hadn't known gay work could actually be printed, I would not have written more. But I kept writing it, nine novels' worth. So it feels only right that I dedicate this collection to you, Patrick. Thanks.

PERRY STREET, GREENWICH VILLAGE

———

I'M OUT ON the front stoop early one evening, talking with our neighbor Cook while I wait for Draper to get home from work. We're continuing an old argument about gay sensibility, something Cook believes all gay men share and I doubt even exists. "If there's a scene in a movie with a lamp in it," says Cook, "a gay man will notice that lamp where a straight man won't." I disagree, citing as evidence two recent conversations about *Vertigo*. The film has an inquest scene where everyone wears suits of the same peculiar shade of phosphorescent blue; nothing in Hitchcock is accidental and it's a puzzling detail. When Draper and I mentioned the suits afterward to the friend who saw the movie with us, that observant gay man said, "What suits?" When I talked about the movie a few days later at the bookstore where I worked, a straight man who'd seen it excitedly asked, "And how about that scene with the weird blue suits?" Cook patiently hears me out, frowns, and says, "I dunno. It'd mean what you think it means if it'd been lamps. Suits are an entirely different animal. Just how straight is this straight man anyway?"

On another night, Draper and I sit on the stoop after dinner, delaying the moment when we climb the five flights to our hot, airless apartment. A man hurries past, then doubles back to ask us something. He's four feet tall, built like a muscular fire hydrant, and grinning with a jumbled mouthful of crooked teeth. His mind races ahead of him on amphetamines. In the course of asking directions to Greenwich Street, he tells us about his happy childhood, unhappy adolescence, battles with a conventional-sized father, and a brief career in midget wrestling that ended when the manager skipped town and stranded the troupe in Florida. "Love to chat, love to jaw with you guys, but I got a hot date and I'm late already, three days late because I had to go to the bank and the cash machine said my mama's check hadn't cleared and I love my mama but her second husband lives out at the track and . . ." He's already halfway down the block, continuing the conversation without us.

Or, on yet another night, very late, I sit alone on the stoop in shorts and black socks, reading tomorrow's *New York Times*. A few cars are backed up at the traffic light in the narrow street. The smoked window of a long limousine suddenly whirs down. "Hey, buddy! Buddy?" A hand comes out of the shadows to point disapprovingly at my feet. "*White* socks. Okay?" The window whirs shut, the light turns green, the limo drives away.

And so on. Most of my neighborhood life seems to take place on the front stoop of our building.

We live in Manhattan, in West Greenwich Village on a side street fifty yards off one of the main avenues. New York City for many people is not so much a place as an abstraction, a frenzied state of mind, an intersection of fast lanes. Home is just a room where you keep your answering machine and go to sleep, a space as private as sleep, often stacked in high-rises with a hundred other private sleeps. You'd go crazy knowing everybody who lives around you, so many New Yorkers prudently screen most of their neighbors out. But there are still real neighborhoods here and there, side streets off the fast lanes. Draper and I have lived here for eleven years. And our building has a stoop.

Seven brown-painted concrete steps climb from a cramped sidewalk to a vestibule full of mailboxes and buzzers. Flanking the steps are two fat concrete walls the color of old chewing gum. The cement flower boxes at the tops of the walls are filled with candy wrappers in the winter and petunias in the spring, diligently tended by our neighbor Peggy and her nine-year-old daughter, Regina. Above the door, caked in flaking nicotine paint, is a droopy stone face with deep-set eyes and a droopy moustache and, above that, the ubiquitous iron zigzag of a fire escape. A five-floor walk-up with sixteen apartments, our building was constructed in 1899, one year after the Spanish-American War and a year before the death of Oscar Wilde. Across the street are older, smaller brick townhouses, very neat and pretty between their cast-iron gates and Federal cornices. There's a similar set of townhouses to the left on our side of the street, thick oak doors shaded by ginkgo trees whose trunks are protected by iron cages. We're probably the ugliest building on the block, but we don't have to look at ourselves when we're on our stoop.

"You got a minute?" asks Cook when I come out and find him sitting there in a Hawaiian shirt, menthol cigarette in one hand, his walking cane hooked over the handrail. "I want to get your opinion on this movie I saw on cable last night—"

Conversation begins with movies, but goes on to political affairs or affairs of the heart or Judyism (Cook doesn't try to convert me to Judy Garland, only explain her cultural importance) or the old Pogo comic strips.

It's chiefly because of Cook and Fred that our stoop is a social institution. I like to think Draper and I helped initiate it, two transplanted Southerners using the front steps as a Yankee equivalent of sociable porches and patios back home. But it's Cook who provides the continuity. He lives on the first floor and the stoop is right outside his door. His narrow apartment is packed with knickknacks, posters, videotapes, books, a ceramic parrot on a perch, all kinds of ashtrays, and over four thousand long-playing records alphabetized by artist—Cook likes music. When he needs a little room to breathe, Cook goes out on the stoop. He knows everybody in the building and half the people in the neighborhood. Those who might be intimidated by Cook's forwardness or strange green eyes (contact lenses, although nobody's supposed to know) are put at ease by Fred. Fred is Cook's dog, a friendly mixture of collie and harp seal with a white face, short snout, and bushy copper coat.

"Sweet dog," say perfect strangers as they walk by and see Fred grinning behind Cook. "You wouldn't say that if you had to live with him," Cook replies. Many stop to pet Fred. By the time they leave they've gotten to know Cook.

Cook is a real New Yorker, Brooklyn bred and born, still lean and quirkily handsome after turning forty. When we first met him, he was a social worker, a city employee who worked with the mentally retarded. He visited families in the outer boroughs, counseling parents, arranging health care and schooling and, sometimes, institutionalization. Cook threw himself completely into his job, even taking kids without families home to his mother's in Brooklyn on holidays. This was before multiple sclerosis tore up his nervous system and damaged his coordination. The MS seems to have stabilized, but Cook walks with a cane now and tires easily. Although he had to leave his job nine years ago, he remains ferociously social. He founded EDGE, Education for a Disabled Gay Environment, a group for lesbians and gay men with physical disabilities, founded the organization because he suddenly wanted to join such a group and discovered no such thing existed. Betrayed by his body, he's more spirited than ever. Cook can get irritable, especially in hot weather when his muscles give out, but I've never heard a word of self-pity from him. He remains stubbornly independent.

One Sunday afternoon, a bedroom-eyed blond chats with Cook for five minutes, then moves on without Cook introducing us. "Who was that?" I ask.

"Crip queen," Cook says contemptuously. "The creep has a fetish for handicaps. He's sleeping his way through EDGE, and I refuse to be another notch on his bedpost. People sleep with me for my sparkling personality," Cook declares, prettily batting his eyes. "Or they don't lay a fucking hand on me."

We're sometimes joined on the stoop by Sam, a large yet graceful man who lives on our floor. Draper calls him Sam the Adult, to distinguish him from Sam the Baby, the two-year-old on the third floor. Sam the Adult smiles a lot with his gopher teeth and walrus moustache, but rarely says much unless the subject is dogs. Sam is enormously sentimental about dogs, far more than Cook. He owns a frisky white mutt named Blanca and is very good friends with Wendy, the equally sentimental dog owner who lives downstairs from him. Wendy was so devoted to her ancient German shepherd, she continued to coax and plead the poor rubber-legged beast up and down the stairs twice a day long after anyone else would've had the animal put to sleep. Wendy is quite old herself, a fact we frequently forget because of her energetic chirp and apparent alertness. She has a petite body and a large head of ghost-white hair. When her dog finally passed away one night on her kitchen floor, it was Sam who carried the bulky animal downstairs in his arms and rode in a cab with Wendy to the veterinarian, indulging her insistence they get an expert opinion before admitting the dog was dead. "Poor Wendy," Sam sighed afterward. "I know just how she feels. You think a dog is forever. Unlike a man."

Straight people are still the majority in the West Village, although just barely. Our landlord is gay, a retired New York City cop who divorced his wife after leaving the force and went at his new life with the fervor of a teenager fresh off the bus. "You *are* one of us?" he proudly asked the first time Draper spoke to him on the phone, about a leak in the roof. Our mailman is gay, I think (he's certainly friendly enough). Most of the people who join us on the stoop are gay, except for Ricki, who lives in the basement with her boyfriend, and Bill.

Bill is Peggy's husband and Regina's father, the family down the hall from me and Draper. Eleven years ago, Bill and Peggy were a bohemian couple, from two different bohemias. A balding, round-faced man with a goatee and motorcycle, Bill was a throwback to the Greenwich Village of the early sixties, coffeehouses and abstract expressionists and folksinging in Washington Square; he supported himself driving a cab. Peggy, with a mimosa stripe of pink in her hair, seemed positively New Wave, all anomie and intellectual paranoia. Everything changed when Regina was born. Bill sold his motorcycle and Peggy became a dedicated Greenwich Village mother, wearing the role like a suit of armor. "We're visiting Regina's friend in Staten Island," she'd tell us on their way out, suggesting her only social life now was her baby daughter's. We've seen Regina grow from a curious infant to a painfully shy toddler to an impossibly arrogant little girl who tromps through us on the stoop in roller skates as if we weren't there. "Regina, don't walk on people," Peggy says indifferently, and continues to water the petunias.

Bill, however, remains friendly and interesting. He started

law school a few years ago but has kept his cabbie's gift for gab. He has street-smart opinions on everything under the sun, from the politics of dumdum bullets to the old Cinema 16 underground movie circuit. "Did I hear someone say *Jackson Pollock?*" he asks when he comes up and hears us talking about a recent biography. "That takes me back to days of yore." And he smiles, puffs up his chest, and delivers a well-informed verdict on action painting. As the oldest married straight man in the building, Bill often plays the role of being everyone's smarter, more practical big brother. If the subjects turns to anything gay, he politely listens a moment before excusing himself with, "Well, gentlemen. Time to trudge up to the wife and family."

Two muscular boys sashay past in those black spandex bicycling shorts that suggest old-time prostitutes in garter belts and hose. All heads turn, but the conversation about *Outweek* and outing continues without missing a beat. Attractive men walk by every hour of the day. A particularly striking one might elicit "Hmmm?" from someone, followed by Cook going, "Nyaah," but further comment would be superfluous.

I hate to admit it, but, when I first moved in with Draper, I was uncomfortable with the prominent numbers of obviously gay men on the street down here. My discomfort was not because of anything like self-hatred or even temptation. It was the unrealness of the situation, the fact that something once secret and rare could become as natural and commonplace as bread. It's not a normal situation, although it should be. I can flip through *Torso* or *Mandate* at the local newsstand (for the book reviews, honest) without fear of a snicker or slur from the Yemenite cousins who own the place. If I run into Draper on his way out and my way in and we exchange a kiss on the stoop, the only reaction we might get is Bill glancing skyward or Sam saying, "Isn't that nice?" as sentimental about us as he is about dogs. There's safety in numbers, and there's the safety that comes of custom. Surrounded by openly gay men and women, straight neighbors take homosexuality for granted and notice only if you're a good neighbor (quiet) or a bad one (noisy). What you do in the privacy of your bedroom is of no interest to anyone else, so long as the bass on your stereo is not turned up too high.

Well, no. Not even the West Village is quite as Arcadian as that. Our neighbors are fine. Visitors can be a problem, especially teenaged boys from Long Island or New Jersey who think the city is a jungle where anything goes. It's homophobia's trickle-down effect, beginning in smug moral pronouncements by clergymen and politicians and ending in insults and sometimes beer cans thrown from car windows late at night. It trickles down even to street people, who've become more numerous on our block over the past two years. Actually, most of the homeless are as indifferent to sexual persuasion as our neighbors with homes, and many are gay themselves. But now and then one sees an angry man scuffing down the sidewalk, muttering, "You faggots make me sick, you faggots make me sick," over and over. Unemployed and homeless, insane or addicted, he must know he's at the bottom of things. But he furiously insists there's someone he can look down on, too.

Other New Yorkers often dismiss the West Village as quaint and unreal, as if familiarity and tolerance were less real than anonymity and threat. Nevertheless, so-called real life comes here, too. There was a crack house on our street, eventually shut down by the police with the neighborhood's cooperation. Not even crack drove us from the stoop, only made us more careful about the strangers we talked to. Our building's garbage cans stand on the sidewalk beside the stoop and conversation is occasionally accompanied by the clink of bottles being sorted into a homeless man's grocery cart. These deposit collectors are too proud to ask for money, although they do sometimes ask for a cigarette.

Draper and I are sitting out front one afternoon with Ricki, who was the building's super before her career as a stage manager took off. A woman with a great swoop of hair above her dirty face stops in front of us, stares at Ricki, and hisses, "You horny little girl! One man isn't enough for you, huh?" Ricki throws her arms around our shoulders and says, "No and it's great!" But the woman has already stomped off to bless out two ten-year-old boys swapping comic books on another stoop down the street. A few days later, I see the woman again, sitting on the pavement outside the Yemenite newsstand, her shirt off and her arms folded over her breasts. "Go ahead and stare!" she screams at passersby. "You perverts! You animals!" A week after that, I spot her shouting at a perplexed Labrador retriever whose leash is tied to a parking meter outside a coffee shop. "You stupid animal! You think you're so smart!"

In such a world, the gender preferences of one's neighbors seem like very small potatoes.

People from other buildings in the neighborhood often stop to talk with us on the stoop. Muriel Spark, author of *The*

Prime of Miss Jean Brodie, owns a co-op in the new brick monstrosity on the corner. She's never sat with us (I wouldn't know her if she bit me), but we are joined by Michael, who works with SAGE at the Lesbian and Gay Community Center a few blocks away. Michael brings us the world of gay bureaucratic squabbles. Then there's Jim from around the corner, a veteran of the old Gay Activist Alliance who remains politically active and savvy, always good for an angle on the news one hasn't heard yet. And there's Tom from next door, an actor and singer who used to perform in children's theater. Now he gives most of his time and energy to the Community Research Initiative, doing staff work for a group of doctors who study alternative AIDS treatments.

"That was a terrific speech you gave at the fund-raiser on Sunday," I tell Tom.

Tom grins sheepishly. "You were there? I'm surprised at all the people I know who showed up. Was a good turnout, wasn't it?"

"Tom gave a speech?" asks Cook.

"Yeah, weelll—" Tom hums and screws up his face in a self-deprecating squinch. "They needed *somebody* from CRI, and old ham that I am . . ."

Much of the talk on the stoop turns around gay politics and the politics of AIDS. Except for Jim, we're not a particularly political bunch, or wouldn't be under normal circumstances. I know Cook would rather discuss the joys of "Be My Baby" by the Ronettes than fume over the latest fatuous statement by John Cardinal O'Connor, but the cardinal's influence is too dangerous to ignore. Draper would prefer to talk about

Bertolucci's forthcoming movie than GLAAD's antiviolence tape, but the tape moved him so much he sent a copy to a friend in Helsinki, who translated and played it on Finnish radio. Tom would rather be a singing cat in a community production of *Pinocchio* than pour over abstracts of AIDS articles in *The New England Journal of Medicine*, but AIDS has become an undeniable part of Tom's life.

Tom's lover died of AIDS two years ago. It was through Stephen, a biochemist, that Tom originally became involved with the Community Research Initiative. And Tom is a PWA himself. He just got out of the hospital again and this week had a catheter lock implanted in his arm for the intravenous treatments he administers to himself. The other day he matter-of-factly explained to me how the lock works, a chemical in a circuit of tube preventing the blood from coagulating over the puncture. We regularly exchange hopes and skepticisms about news in the *Times, New York Native,* and *Village Voice.* Within a week after coming home from the hospital, Tom resumed going to the CRI offices for meetings. Cook, who has no pity for himself, thinks Tom has a right to some self-pity and can't understand why he won't indulge, just a little. I feel awed and shamed by both of them.

Journalists with a melodramatic bent describe the West Village in the age of AIDS as "devastated" and "the killing fields." A young writer who should have known better did a piece about walking his dog in a gay ghost town. The West Village isn't any of those things. Gay life goes on, everyday and commonplace life. Attractive men still notice each other on the street, although they're not as quick to go home together as they once were; there's more conversation nowadays, more flirtation. On our stoop, we continue to talk about old movies and Motown's greatest hits, but we also talk about AIDS and politics. We run into each other at memorial services (Stephen's was in a chapel one block away) and protest rallies. I was startled to realize how much "in the life" I am, and how political that life has become, when I went to a mammoth ACT UP demonstration at city hall last year and could not turn around without seeing someone I knew among the protesters circling the park in an endless conga line of chanters and placards. Squads of mounted police covered the approaches to the Brooklyn Bridge in the distance, epic and ominous in the hazy morning light, but up close all I saw were friends and neighbors.

I don't know how much thought my straight neighbors give to AIDS. The young couples appear well informed and somewhat concerned. The older people seem to block the topic completely from their minds. The sentiment of "Love thy neighbor" is not as effective in keeping the peace as that other American adage, "Mind your own business," which means tolerance sometimes shades into a careful indifference. In our building, twenty-three very different people live over a plot of ground that might be enough for a single nuclear family in the suburbs. A hundred different wars, some more private than others, take place simultaneously here. We don't share the same wars. We don't even watch the same TV shows. Although recently, when Wagner's *Ring* was televised over four nights, I was amazed to come up the stairs the first night and hear the muffled sound of *Das Rheingold* on each and every floor. Behind Cook's door Judy Garland sang a duet with Mickey Rooney, but everyone else seemed to be trying a taste of Wagner. It was both comic and spooky. By the last night, *Götterdämmerung* was heard only on the third and fifth floors, but for a few hours the entire building finally had something in common.

Actually, there was one other shared experience, an incident that involved more of us than anything else that's happened here. I have to change details and the identity of one of the participants so nobody will get in trouble, but the spirit of the story is true.

Wendy, the cheerful white-haired woman who lost her German shepherd, lived on the third floor. A nephew sometimes stayed with her, a gaunt, morose fellow who wore eyeglasses as thick as his aunt's. Wendy was alone one evening when a lamp in her bedroom shorted out, starting a fire in the bed that sat on the wiring. Filling a pan with water, Wendy quickly extinguished the fire herself. She *thought* she extinguished it, anyway. The short had blown a fuse and her lights were out. It was getting dark, but Wendy expected her nephew that evening and did not want to trouble her neighbors. She sat there in the dark with her two cats and patiently waited for the nephew to arrive.

Draper and I smelled smoke in the halls when we went out for dinner. We passed Peggy coming up the stairs from Wendy's floor. Ever since she became a mother, Peggy has been keenly alert to every sinister noise or smell in the building. "I just checked," she told us. "Wendy said she burned something, but everything's okay."

When Sam came home a half hour later, there was still smoke in the hall. He knocked on Wendy's door and asked if she were all right. "Everything's fine, thank you," Wendy called through the closed door. Sam went upstairs.

When Draper and I returned from dinner, the smoke still lingered, a smell of burnt protein, like meat. The ventilation in all the kitchens is bad; we know every night exactly what our downstairs neighbors are having for dinner. Mildly nervous, yet familiar with the building's idiosyncrasies and ashamed of our nervousness, we settled down in our apartment to watch television.

It was Bill, the ex–cab driver, the building's know-it-all big brother, who finally did something. He went down to Wendy's and banged furiously on her door.

"Sorry if I alarmed anyone," Wendy called out. "But everything's fine now."

"Everything is *not* fine!" Bill declared. "The hall's been full of smoke for two hours. Let me in right this minute."

She guiltily opened the door and Bill saw the pitch-black apartment. In the light from the hall, he saw the thin haze of smoke inside, then the blackened mattress.

"Jesus, Mary, and Joseph!"

"I put it out with a pan of water," Wendy explained.

"The hell you did! The wadding in these things burns forever. Can't you see? It's still burning!"

We heard Bill shouting in the stairwell. Then the smell of smoke was suddenly very strong. We ran out to the hall, looked over the rail, and saw Bill and Sam dragging a smoking, blackened mattress down the stairs. The mattress left a trail of smeared ashes on the steps and landings, and flakes of charred cloth like black leaves.

Nobody called the fire department. The fire was all in the bed and everyone agreed the water damage would be far worse than a stink of smoke in the halls. More important, if the fire department were called in, then the landlord would learn what had happened. The consensus, gay and straight, is that Danny's a decent fellow, but he's still a landlord.

"I'm not saying he'd actually do it," Bill argued when he and Sam returned from the street. "But I wouldn't put it past Danny to evict Wendy for this stunt, saying she's too senile to stay here, that she's a hazard to his tenants. And it would give him one more rent-controlled apartment he could put on the open market."

Almost immediately, Sam was out on the stairs with a broom, sweeping up all evidence of fire, Draper following him with a dustpan and trash bag. Bill and I hunted inside Wendy's apartment with flashlights, looking for her fuse box. Wendy couldn't remember where it was and suggested we call the electrician who installed the outside line for her air conditioner. Hearing her air conditioner was on a different circuit, I plugged a lamp into that outlet and we suddenly had light.

"Oh Jesus," groaned Bill. "Will you look at this?" We almost never see the insides of each other's apartments. Wendy's was full of stacked newspapers and magazines, collapsed piles that covered her floor with paper. The windows were shut tight to keep her cats from getting out; one cat shyly watched us from under a sofa heaped with health brochures. Wendy stood by the sink, not in the slightest bit upset or frightened, her eyeglasses slightly askew.

Bill kept his temper. "I don't know if you realize it, Wendy. But I just saved your life," he sternly told her. "With that mattress still going and your windows shut, you would've died of asphyxiation if I hadn't come when I did. I don't even want to think about what might've happened next."

The box spring the mattress sat on was charred on one side. I touched it and felt heat, a slow burning in the wooden frame. Bill and I carried the box spring downstairs to the street.

"I got my wife and daughter to think about," Bill said as we maneuvered down the corkscrew of stairs. "But I don't want to see that little old lady evicted either. If she were thrown out on the street, she'd end up homeless, I know she would. We're going to have to work out something with her nephew."

We set the box spring outside on the curb next to the mattress. The mattress continued to smolder, a smoking slab of springs and stuffing. At that moment, Cook came hopping up the sidewalk on his cane, coming home from a meeting at the Center. "Ohhh shit," he said. "Who's gone and done what now?"

Bill returned upstairs and I told Cook what happened. "That Wendy," Cook sighed, and filled pots of water at his sink which I carried outside to douse the mattress and box spring. Bill was right: beds burn forever.

Sam and Draper came out the door, sweeping the last of the ashes in front of them. We all stood on the stoop, looking down at the scorched bed in the gutter. "Looks like somebody still has hot sex," Cook muttered, then twitched his eyebrows wickedly and added, "I didn't really say that."

We disposed of the extinguished mattress and box spring that night. An electrician came the next day and made Wendy's wiring safe again. Her nephew bundled up the newspapers and magazines and cleaned out the apartment. This all happened several years ago and Wendy was not evicted, our building has not burned down.

1992

A BODY IN BOOKS:
A MEMOIR IN A
READING LIST

—w—

*All art **may be** sublimated sexuality,*
*but **then** so is all sexuality.*

—ADAM PHILLIPS

T HE CULTURE AT large regularly instructs
people on how to be heterosexual.
Movies, television, popular music, and advertising are about almost nothing else. But gay
men and women, at least until recently, have
had only books to help them find or invent
or test their identities. A college professor
recently wrote that a gay identity is often a literary construct, which set me thinking about
the books that I read on my way to who I am.
What were they? How did I read them? What
did I take from these words and stories?

This is an experiment in literary self-criticism, a memoir in a reading list, an autobibliography. All gay readers have their own lists of titles; I expect mine will make you think about yours.

Before I list the books, I should sketch in some prehistory.

I loved books before I loved bodies. The bodies didn't appear until junior high. Gay identity might not be biological, but I believe homosexual lust is. Mine certainly was. It first expressed itself as a simple desire to see other boys naked. I thought I'd enjoy seeing anyone naked, and told myself that I took special pleasure in boys only because there were no girls in the locker room or on Scout camping trips. The first indication that my tastes were more specific came when I was fourteen and discovered the photoplates of Greek sculpture in my grandmother's 1920s edition of the *Encyclopedia Britannica*. I found more depth and magic in the rectangular bulk of the male nudes than in the smoother, rounder female beauties.

I'm not sure where I first saw the word *homosexual*. *Time* magazine? I don't remember the title of the psychology paperback I stumbled upon in Beacon Bookstore in Norfolk, Virginia, that gave me my first useful piece of information: most adolescents go through a homosexual phase. Which put my mind at ease, allowing me to think about naked boys without guilt while I pursued such wholesome, all-American activities as delivering the morning paper, earning Boy Scout merit badges, and taking Latin so I could read the footnotes in *The Decline and Fall of the Roman Empire*.

I was, in fact, a strange kid, solitary and private, not lonely but cheerfully self-sufficient, bookish without being literary.

For years I read nothing but military history, dry accounts of tactics and strategy, violence made safe and bloodless. There was no public library nearby, the high school library was understocked, and the nearest bookstore was in Norfolk, an hour away. I had a recurring dream where I came upon a bookcase full of titles I hadn't read or even heard of. I'd wake up eager to inspect these books, only to realize that they didn't exist.

So books were as magical to me as male bodies. I am still trying to understand how the two magics connect. I did not discover fiction until I was thirteen, at roughly the same time that I discovered my own body. I cannot remember which came first, reading novels or sleeping nude, but I suddenly enjoyed being naked in bed, all skin and bedclothes—I didn't discover masturbation until a year later. And I enjoyed the bodies in novels. Military history offers only corpses, but novels are full of live flesh: a boy swims naked in the first pages of *The Lord of the Flies* by William Golding, Polynesians guiltlessly drop their sarongs in *Hawaii* by James Michener, freezing Yankee prisoners clutch each other for warmth in *Andersonville* by MacKinley Kantor. I continued to read history, but there too I was finding less abstract, more physical experience. *A Stillness at Appomattox* by Bruce Catton showed me just how much could be done with prose, conjuring up the look and smell of landscapes, campfires, and battlefields with firsthand richness and immediacy.

Soon I was reading Fitzgerald, Hemingway, and Dreiser, the brand names of literature, with varying degrees of satisfaction. And then I began to stumble upon books that enabled me to connect the polymorphous joys of reading with the more specific, unnamed excitement of the body.

1. *An End to Innocence* by Leslie Fiedler.

The title is too appropriate. I am still amazed that I read Fiedler so early, when I was sixteen. But his essays about the Rosenbergs and Alger Hiss meant nothing to me. No, what I found startling was a piece titled "Come Back to the Raft Ag'in, Huck Honey."

It was 1968, my first year as a counselor at Camp Kiwanis, a Boy Scout camp on the James River. One rainy morning all activities were suspended and I hung out with other counselors in the staff lounge, a cinderblock hut with a cement floor. Someone—I never discovered who—had left a battered paperback on the mattress we used as a sofa. I picked it up, noticed an essay on *Huckleberry Finn*, and immediately began to read, simply because it was about literature. One didn't get much literature at Camp Kiwanis. But these pages went deeper than mere books.

"Come Back to the Raft" is the notorious essay where Fiedler first proposed that a dominant theme of American literature is the flight of the white man from female civilization in the arms of a dusky male lover: Huck and Jim, Natty Bumpo and Chingachook, Ishmael and Queequeg. Fiedler never comes right out and calls them homosexuals, but uses the gentler, more chaste word—to my eye, anyway—*homoerotic.* What he's actually saying, and makes clearer in *Love and Death in the American Novel,* is that this is a failing of American literature, which is crippled by a disdain for healthy heterosexual love.

But that wasn't noticed by a skinny Scout in glasses, green shorts, and knee socks who sat reading on the mattress with his mouth half open. What struck and amazed me—and I wondered if I were reading it correctly—was the discovery that my crushes and curiosities—my fondness for Stevie S. and desire to see him naked—were not just peculiar to me or a sickness I shared with a few perverts, but a major theme of American literature, as American as Huck Finn.

2. *Thomas Mann.*

This prim, erudite, stiff-collared German was my first serious literary hobbyhorse. It began as pure pose. I was drawn to Mann by his reputation as an important cultural figure—I was bent on improving myself. The rumor of *Death in Venice* was tucked away somewhere in my curiosity, of course, but the first time I read the novella—on the sly in the Norfolk Public Library—I found the story dry and boring. No, the works that moved me were *Buddenbrooks* and *The Magic Mountain*.

One of the most intense literary experiences of my life was the Friday evening when I read the Hanno section of *Buddenbrooks* in our kitchen, completely losing myself in Hanno's day—a typical school day circa 1890, so similar yet so different from my own life. When I finished, I couldn't remember what day I was actually in, if it were a school night or not. I followed Hans Castorp through all seven hundred pages of *The Magic Mountain*, his leisurely education in a sanitorium. I finished the novel late one night around Christmas and wandered our sleeping house in a daze, stunned by the author's farewell to the young man stumbling over a battlefield, singing Schubert to himself, Mann claiming we shouldn't care if Hans lives or dies, his story is over.

It didn't hurt that Mann was so matter-of-fact about boys

falling in love with boys: Hanno with Kai, Hans Castorp with Pribislav Hippe, Tonio Kroger with Hans Hansen. Which was exactly as the psychology book said: many adolescents go through a homosexual phase. Because a Nobel Prize–winner treated such crushes as natural, I accepted mine as not just normal, but literary and artistic.

This fascination with Mann continued through college. I wrote two papers about him for a favorite teacher in German history, following Mann's tacking back and forth against the winds of change. I fell in love with my own Hans Castorps, boy-next-door chatterboxes who mixed normalcy with promising curiosity. I openly referred to one as "life's delicate child"—as Castorp is called in the Lowe-Porter translation—and noticed another had "Kirghiz eyes," like Castorp's male and female beloveds, Hippe and Claudia.

When I visited Swiss relatives in 1976, in the village of Kilchberg, I was thrilled to learn that my Uncle Arthur had designed the cemetery where Mann now rests—my family had touched literary greatness, if only to bury it. My uncle is now interred twenty yards from the *Dichter*. I was done with Mann, however, by the time his diaries were published and the world learned that homosexual love was not just a metaphor in his fiction but central to his life. A gay German who met my boy-friend at the beach told us about the diaries one night over dinner, and I thought: Of course. Why hadn't I realized that?

3. *The Counterfeiters* by André Gide.

I'm not sure what made me take this book from the library at Kempsville High School when I was seventeen, what, if anything, I knew about Gide except that he was "important." But from the very first pages I was swept up in its quick, brisk prose; its game of pairing this character with that one, the author shuffling people like cards; and its tales of adolescent boys. What thrilled me most was an early scene where Bernard shares a bed with his friend Olivier, and wakes up to find Olivier pressed against him with one arm weighing "indiscreetly upon his flesh." Later episodes feature love between men and boys—Olivier attempts suicide after sex with his uncle (very elliptical sex), not from shame but joy—and a pack of younger boys form a secret society around masturbation and Russian roulette. But it was the scene of Bernard and Olivier sharing a bed that stayed with me for years, giving my desire its first clear target. Whenever I fell in love with someone, all I could imagine was sleeping with him, one arm laid "indiscreetly upon his flesh."

I first read that chapter in study hall and promptly showed it to the young, blond acquaintance sitting beside me, my Hans Castorp of the season. I shared it as a joke, a gross-out, yet hoped he'd be intrigued. He was only grossed out. But I'd discovered a new use for literature, not only for reading my own desires, but for reading the desires of others, testing their interest without fully exposing mine.

4. *Good Times, Bad Times* by James Kirkwood.

We take what we need where we find it, and commercial fiction often speaks louder than literature. This 1968 novel was first shown to me in study hall—we seemed to do a lot of reading in study hall—by Laura Leigh B., a tomboyish folksinger in my church youth group. It's a prep school novel where the chaste romantic friendship of two boys is treated as clean and beautiful, in contrast to the dirty lust of the closeted headmaster. Late in the book, the headmaster gets drunk and gives the narrator a backrub. The boy pretends to be asleep while the man spills rubbing alcohol on his back, works his way down, then pulls off his pajama bottoms. The boy keeps his eyes squeezed shut and tries to will away his erection. It was the sexiest thing I'd ever read.

This was the scene that Laura Leigh showed me in study hall, much as I'd shown that boy a page in Gide. I was too electrified by the rubdown, however, to wonder what Laura Leigh was testing. I feigned mild amusement, returned the book to her, then went to the shopping mall the next day and bought my own copy.

Good Times, Bad Times is another of those gay stories where one of the lovers must die before the story ends—here it's a conveniently weak heart, if I remember right. But I knew that was only for the sake of the story; I believed that two boys could love each other without either one dropping dead. Unconconsciously, however, the novel may have reinforced my feeling that homosexual love was fine, but sex was wrong. Here was a tale where one man's love for another was acceptable so long as he didn't do anything "dirty" with it. You might literally sleep with the beloved, but blowjobs were evil. ("Blowjob" had such an ugly sound back then. If some words enabled me to accept my crushes without guilt, others prevented me from thinking about actual sex.)

5. *Oscar Wilde.*

This was not one book but a whole cluster, read for the term paper that I wrote in my senior English class, "Oscar Wilde: The Artist as Homosexual."

I got away with it because of my reputation as class clown, the fellow who'd say anything to shock people. Laura Leigh volunteered to type it for me so she'd get a chance to read it. (What exactly was Laura Leigh's story? She later worked at the church camp where my sister worked, down river from my Scout camp. She scandalized the more priggish girls by having an openly sexual affair with one of the male counselors. Laura Leigh appeared to have had a healthily transgressive soul.)

I read *The Picture of Dorian Gray*, a couple of plays, some essays, two biographies, and a general study of the "Homosexuality: Threat or Menace" variety. I discovered the giddily absurd logic of *The Importance of Being Earnest* and picked up a few one-liners that continue to pepper my speech—"We are all in the gutter, but some of us are looking at stars." I was much taken with one biographer's claim that Wilde's favorite sexual activity was to have a naked male prostitute sit in his lap, which sounded like fun. (The biographer said this was very revealing psychologically—only he never said what it revealed.) For my paper's cover sheet, I drew a copy of the Max Beerbohm cartoon of Wilde dripping with chins and jewelry—as if to insist that I could never identify with such a man. I regret to say that the paper's thesis was something along the lines of "Yes, Wilde was a homosexual, but it's okay, because he also wrote *The Importance of Being Earnest.*"

6. *The Red and the Black* by Stendhal.

One can learn from the most unexpected sources, and you sometimes find knowledge aslant, with a detour through reality.

Back at summer camp, at eighteen, I read Stendhal after reading Leslie Fiedler again, *Love and Death in the American Novel* this time. I wanted to follow up on his claim that Americans don't do mature, heterosexual love as well as the Europeans. *The Red and the Black* is nothing if not hetero. Julian Sorel, a handsome young priest, has a friend back home whose devotion struck me as awfully Huck-like, but Julian himself pursues only women. He courts a married provincial woman, then a neurotic rich girl, then shoots the married woman and is sent to the guillotine. I couldn't understand why this was more mature than *Huckleberry Finn* but nevertheless loved the novel. I was fascinated by Stendhal's wry dissection of love as a game, half real, half invented, a constellation of emotions unlimited by moral convention.

I was in love that summer with Al W. Al was not one of my bland Hans Castorps, but lively, quirky, unpredictable. A year younger than me, he was a navy brat from a Catholic family, small for his age, with a head too big for his bony body. He compensated for his size with wildness and noise, yet without shutting out his basic decency or sweetness. We'd known each other for years, first in our Scout troop, then in school where we hung out with friends in the library. But that summer, for some reason, we began to flirt.

There is no other word for it. I cannot guess what triggered our mutual curiosity, but we timed our showers so we took them together, amiably chatting side by side, then prolonged our intimacy while we dried off and got dressed. At night we'd get together to watch television and Al would set a folded tarp on the office floor and invite me to lie beside him.

I'd just read Stendhal's description of the hand game that Julian plays with Madame Renal in a dark garden. Will she let me touch her? Will she let me hold her hand? Stendhal makes it as suspenseful as a bank robbery. I began to play a similar game with Al. Can I set my hand by his? Will he move his hand away? What if I set my hand by his thigh? What if I brush his knee? This went on for several nights, a whole week in fact, as I worked up my nerve and inched my way toward expressing what I couldn't say in words. Until finally, I set my hand on his hip, just so, palm over the hipbone, fingers in the shallow bowl of his middle . . . and Al took my hand, returned it to my lap, frowned and shook his head, and resumed watching television.

This was my first attempt to express my love for another guy. And yes, it was subtle, but I'd at least made the attempt. Al and I remained friends, and we continued to flirt, and I went even further. But that's another story and has nothing to do with literature.

7. *Tike and Five Stories* by Jonathan Strong.

There was a short story here that once meant the world to me, "Supperburger."

It was my freshman year at the College of William and Mary and I finally had access to a good library. I prowled the stacks there, looking for new fiction that would teach me how to write. I discovered "Supperburger" in an O. Henry

Prize anthology, which led me to Strong's own book. There was another story in *Tike* I liked, "Saying Goodbye to Tom," where two friends fall asleep together "like little kids," but "Supperburger" was a bullet to my heart.

A street boy, Patrick Polo, goes home one night with a married composer, Arthur Supperburger, while the man's wife is away. Supperburger later invites Patrick back for dinner, with his wife and a cute nephew, a college student named Louie. He tells Patrick that he can never see him again. Heartbroken, Patrick goes off for a walk with Louie, the two boys talking late into the night.

I'm not sure why the story meant so much to me. Except for a mention of hickeys on Patrick's neck, there is nothing overtly sexual. Perhaps it was just a story I needed to hear at the time. Its world was closer to the world I knew firsthand than any other gay tale I'd come across, one of students and townies and sixties street life. And nobody dies in it. The love between men is not treated as sinister, but as tender, sad, with the suggestion that love might work for Patrick and Louie. The story is quiet and clear, yet unashamedly romantic.

I wrote Strong a fan letter, saying I wanted to meet him if I hitchhiked up to Boston at the end of the summer. When I didn't hear back from him, I went hiking instead on the Appalachian Trail with Al, after a brief stop in Washington to visit his new girlfriend.

I read Strong's next book, a novel, *Ourselves*, and was sorely disappointed that it was not about "that stuff," but a heterosexual love story. (I didn't use the word *gay* back then, or even *homosexual*. I had no name for my cluster of romantic feelings.) But I continued to reread "Supperburger." At one point, unable to live the story, I daydreamed about making a movie of it, starring Bob M., a mild crush of the time.

The books that are most important to us are not always famous works of literature. In a list of favorite authors that I scribbled for myself my sophomore year, I cited Tolstoy, Stendhal, Proust, and Jonathan Strong.

Much later, after I published my first novel, I finally met Strong. He turned out to be gay, although it took him fifteen years after "Supperburger" to write about "that stuff" again. He did not remember getting a love letter disguised as fan mail from a nineteen-year-old in Virginia.

8. *Remembrance of Things Past* by Marcel Proust.

I attempted to climb this mountain range in high school, but could not make head or tail of it. Unable to picture the clothes or furniture, I wasn't even sure what century it took place in. But, sophomore year in college, I read it, the whole damn thing. It took me the entire year, with a break in the middle for something lighter, *Anna Karenina*.

Proust was profoundly important to me—he remains important—although not for his detailed account of gay underground life. Even then I did not believe his famous chapter about Sodom in *Cities of the Plain* (this was the Scott Moncrieff translation). All I took from those bleak pages was the story of two friends in the country who meet at a crossroads one night and make love in the grass. One man marries, the other doesn't, but both live unhappy, dishonest lives. I didn't care about their unhappiness, however. I just wanted a friend who'd meet me at the crossroads, which I pictured as a moonlit country lane at Camp Kiwanis.

No, what I learned from Proust, what I took from his book that shaped my understanding of love—and my sexuality— was his recognition of the "mentalness" of the world, the elasticity of reality, a poetry of deep subjective space. I'm not sure how to explain it. I didn't fully recognize the sensibility until ten years later, when I reread the monster in the revised translation by Terence Kilmartin and saw how much my feelings about love and reality had been shaped by Proust. Perhaps it can be best summed up by the idea that the great dramas of life are all interior.

Which is a dangerous way to think. It can send you tumbling down the rabbit hole of self. It can lock you in the closet with all your pretty emotions. I was thrilled by the new colors this Proustian poetry added to my infatuations, the literary halo it gave to such stupid acts as following Kevin What's-His-Name, a sullen, nerdy accounting major, across campus without him seeing me. I knew Kevin was nobody's romantic ideal, not even my own. But infatuation wasn't objective. It was my creation, a work of art far more exciting than the short stories I was writing. The trick, of course, is to get your story to write a similar story about you, which is not damned likely.

Now that I think of it, the year I read Proust was my most melancholy time since the onset of puberty, and the most repressed. It was also the year that I started sleeping with women. Proust was a retreat into the self, a huge step backward, but perhaps one that I needed before I could finally take a leap forward.

9. *Black Mountain: An Exploration in Community* by Martin Duberman.

This study of the Black Mountain School in North Carolina created an enormous stir when it appeared in 1972, not for its story of an experiment in education, but because its author included a few details about himself, among them the fact that he was gay. After reading one enraged reviewer in the *New York Times*, I burned to read the book, which I checked out of the local public library while home over Christmas. But homosexuality, Duberman's as well as that of Paul Goodman and other teachers at Black Mountain, occupied only a few scant pages. Nevertheless, I found the book fascinating. I never knew that the history of an institution of learning could be made as exciting as a military campaign.

I was drawn to *Black Mountain* by sex, but found something else instead. In the course of that detour, I made an important discovery. Homosexuality is not off in its own universe, an isolated island, but connects with the rest of life. It can inform and color such diverse activities as teaching, poetry, politics, architecture, painting. Looking back, I'm surprised I didn't already know that. At the time, I seemed to think being homosexual was a full-time profession, an all-encompassing identity that allowed no room for anything else.

10. *End as a Man* by Calder Willingham.

I went on a gay reading binge the summer after I graduated, when I stayed in town to work as a projectionist at the college. The audiovisual department was in the library basement. Between screenings, I returned to the stacks upstairs, no longer looking for books about love, but books about sex. I suddenly needed to imagine sex with a man, in all its lurid details, so I could want it badly enough to risk asking for it. The few bits of porn I'd encountered were badly written absurdities with too many food metaphors. I wanted sex scenes that were literary yet graphic, mixing skin and emotion, obscene acts and good prose.

I read all the usual suspects. I recognized that *A Single Man* by Christopher Isherwood was a fine novel, but I wanted a good fuck scene—the drunken nude swim was too much like the fantasies I already had. *The City and the Pillar* by Gore Vidal had some hot sex between two teenagers in its opening pages, but went downhill from there. After years of longing, Jim, the protagonist, finally meets up again with his beloved, only to find the guy is straight. So he kills him. (This was the original 1948 edition. In his 1965 revision, Vidal relented and Jim merely rapes the poor guy.) This was not the erotic drama I wanted for myself.

The Calder Willingham novel wasn't what I wanted either: dark sado-homo doings in a Southern military academy. My Freudian memory insists on misremembering the title as *Enter a Man.* Yet the book gave me something else. The margins of the library copy, an original edition from 1947, were full of notes penciled by a previous reader, a running argument with the text: "Oh please," or "Get out of here." On the page where the villain finally tells the remarkably obtuse hero, "I am a practicing homosexual," my predecessor had written, "Oh, Calder. How shocking!" I couldn't guess how old his comments were, but I was tickled to learn that other gay men had read these books. And the comments were not merely skeptical, but mocking, scornful. Just because something was in print didn't mean that we should believe it—I now saw that I could be part of a "we."

11. *The Story of Harold* by Terry Andrews.

This remarkable novel has a cult following, but should be better known. Published under a pseudonym in 1974 (rumored to be by George Selden, author of such children's classics as *The Cricket in Times Square*), it's ostensibly the diary of a children's author named Terry Andrews, a bisexual man who is exploring S&M. (He *says* he's bisexual, but all his encounters are with men.)

I stumbled upon the novel in a university bookstore in Madison, Wisconsin, where I was visiting my best friend, a woman who knew I was gay, but was unhappily in love with me. We went to bed during the visit, which only added to my guilt that I couldn't return her love. I began to read *The Story of Harold* on the long train ride home to Virginia.

The book gave me the sex scenes that I craved, with a vengeance. Not only is there fucking, rough sex, and an orgy, there are luxuriant descriptions of fisting, "like putting your fingers in fold upon fold of hot, wet velvet, some fabric never felt before, that contains a living pulse within it." I was twenty-three. I'd been to bed with my first man only the month before. Yet here I was, reading about an act so dangerously intimate it left me weak in the knees. It did not give me a taste for sadism or fisting, but dissolved any taboos I had left, prying my imagination wide open.

And I was opened up to the emotional power of the book,

its startling juxtapositions. Terry is in love with a happily married doctor. Terry plays "master" in their encounters, but it's clear who the real master is. There is also a social worker, an Irish Catholic whose masochism is not just role-playing but full of real pain and self-hatred. Chapters about sex alternate with chapters about the new children's story Terry is creating for the sake of a troubled six-year-old boy who's been left in his care.

The book taught me something as a writer: mixing the obscene and the mundane can create fresh energy and complex truths. *Harold* explores the relation of sex to the rest of life, its simultaneous continuity and discontinuity with the world outside a bed. A good fuck is not always an escape from daily life, but a heightening of it, reality carried on by other means.

This is not just a writing lesson, of course, but questions of technique often blend into questions about how we live.

12. *The Other Persuasion* edited by Seymour Kleinberg.

This 1977 anthology includes a wide range of fiction about gay life, from outside observers like Faulkner and Hemingway to insiders like Cather and Purdy. I first encountered Edmund White here, in a short story called "The Beautiful Room Is Empty," unrelated to his later novel of that title. I liked it well enough, but the key story for me was one by Jane Rule, "Middle Children."

Two young women from large families, so-called middle children (said to be better adjusted than first- or last-born), meet in college and fall in love, easily and naturally, without a speck of guilt. When they set up house together, however, they find that romantic love is not enough. Isolation puts a strain on their bond. So they get a bigger house, rent out rooms, and make themselves part of a large, changing family of straight and gay people. They are very happy.

I was back in Virginia after spending six months in Europe, back in Williamsburg and living with the straight man whom I'd been in love with for three years. I was finally having sex with other men. Not often enough, and not without complications, nor with anyone I loved, though I liked my partners well enough. I needed to know if it were possible to integrate sexual love into the rest of life. Jane Rule said it's not only possible, but necessary.

Her story is so simple, an idyll, a fairy tale with a few realistic details to anchor it to earth. That pluralistic household could never be achieved as easily as Rule's narrator tells it. And yet, it is pretty to think so, a hope worth having, a fantasy worth wanting.

13. *Surprising Myself* by Christopher Bram.

Yes, this is my own novel, a book that I wrote. But if reading is often misreading—rewriting if you will—writing can be a deeper, more active form of reading. In the words of E. M. Forster's old lady, "How can I know what I think until I see what I say?" And that was true of my novel.

I worked on it for seven years, producing three drafts of a book nearly twice as long as the one I finally published in 1987. I'd written an earlier novel, a straight story that I was never able to sell. Since this one might go unpublished, too, I decided to write what I wanted to write, which meant writing about homosexuality.

But I knew gay life was a hard sell and I worked out a narrative strategy: my narrator, Joel Scherzenlieb, is a neoconservative twit who doesn't become fully human until he comes out. The idea was that even straight readers would want him to accept his homosexuality—as if there'd be any straight readers, or that anyone would stick with Joel for three hundred pages before he became human. These are the pages that I later cut.

You start a book with clear purpose and preconceptions, then find your story taking you places you hadn't intended. The novel was never consciously autobiographical. Joel wasn't me—my parents were still married, I'd *never* been a Republican. He was the bland yet promising type of boy I used to fall in love with, an American Hans Castorp. And yet, sometime during the writing, Joel became me, or maybe I became him. A year into the first draft, I met my boyfriend, Draper, who's nothing like Hans Castorp, God bless him. Requited love changed my story from a halfhearted comedy about coming out to a more rueful, complex comedy about living in a couple, the slipperiness of domestic love, the kind of love that Joel's lover, Corey, calls, after Laurence Sterne, "not so much an emotion as a situation."

Their situation leaves them open to other lives: Joel's quasihippie mother on a farm in Virginia, his sister Liza and her bad marriage to an army officer, his flaky father who quits the CIA to become an actor. I gave the book a wild mix solely for dramatic reasons, to keep things lively. Putting together this list of books, however, I see that the mix was not just about storytelling, but about the kind of life that I'd learned to want through my reading: a gay life, but one that connects to other worlds, as it does in Martin Duberman and Jane Rule; and a conscious life, one that does not repress the dark erotics of Terry Andrews, but where the deep interior space of Proust can be occasionally escaped in provisional, requited love.

That's a lot to load on a first novel and might be why *Surprising Myself* is so messy. I've written better books since. But by writing it, I was able to finish what Mann and Proust and the other books began, coming up with my own answers to the questions they'd raised. They were only temporary answers, of course, but those are the best kind.

So there we have it, thirteen reading experiences that helped to make me who I am.

Mayor Jimmy Walker of New York once said that no girl was ever ruined by a book. Did books ruin me? Or did they save me? Would I have let myself fall in love with boys if Thomas Mann hadn't given my crushes a literary stamp of approval? Would I have continued my hand game with Al if I hadn't read *The Red and the Black*? Maybe not, although desire would have found other outlets, in time. I sometimes get letters from grown men who say, "If only I'd read your novel when I was fourteen, I might have found myself sooner." But would they?

Looking over this list, I cannot say that I was "constructed" by these books. I used them as tools to construct myself, much as a monkey uses whatever object is handy to get what he wants. But the tool can change the nature of his wanting, making it broader or more precise. I was not a blank slate, a passive receptacle for stories. Consciously as well as unconsciously, I entered into a dialogue with these books. More accurately, I used them as an occasion to address my sexuality, a safe place where I could daydream and try out different roles in sex and love. The reader brings a lot to the party, picking and choosing what he or she needs, ignoring the rest.

So who is the person these books helped to create? A gay man who writes gay novels, of course, but also someone who wants a homosexuality that connects with as much life as possible. If I sometimes read with my dick, it must be said that a hard cock isn't always the proverbial blinding beam in the eye. It can be a pointer, a compass needle, a divining rod.

I was not just a body; I was a body among books. Books have meant the world to me ever since childhood, when they were magic objects, physical yet dreamlike. I still have a tactile fetish for books, which some might give an autoerotic interpretation—a mass market paperback fits so nicely in the hand. But books *are* like bodies, solid matter full of inner life, intellect, and emotion. There was a time when sex and reading seemed identical for me. I wanted to undress a book to its bare meaning; I wanted to "read" men naked.

A book can be so many things. In public it's a little placard, a declaration of your beliefs and fantasies. Or, without its jacket, it can be a handheld privacy, a portable closet. Readers are a curious species, a strange minority; gay readers are a minority within a minority. The psychology of reading remains to be written, a mild pathology of pleasure, sublimation, deferral, and transference. Yet books offer the most diverse set of tools for an individual to find his or her self. I am prejudiced here, but I believe literature provides a looser, broader, more varied medium in which to explore one's identity than movies or television do—even now as gay and lesbian images make their way into mass media.

I read my way into homosexuality, which may be why I became a writer. If somewhere along the line, a nice attractive guy had seen through my arrogance and taken me to bed, perhaps my sexuality wouldn't have gotten tangled up in literature. I may have become the lawyer that my parents wanted. Or maybe not. The love of books was already stamped into my being, like my love of boys.

I lost myself in a forest of books. I took my sweet time before I found my way out again. Some might say that I am still lost in the woods. Yet a remarkable variety of experience can reach you in the shelter of the trees. The light is softer and there are more shades of gray; the world looks less black-and-white. The self produced by these books wouldn't have it any other way.

2000

SLOW
LEARNERS

—w—

1

I WENT TO COLLEGE in a quaint, damp,
green Virginia town, where I spent four
years falling in love with men and going to
bed with women. There were many men—
usually a new one each semester—and only
a few women.

I already suspected I was homosexual, but
in a detached, oblivious sort of way. Falling in
love with anyone was such a relief for a boy
who feared he was cold and heartless that the

skew of my affection didn't panic me. I told nobody and worried only over what to do with my nervous elation. Sex seemed a good idea, except I was physically attracted only to men I fell in love with, and love made me too respectful to propose anything so rude. There was no terror of being odd, no hunger for normalcy, no conscious guilt—nothing worse than a fear of scaring off the other person. Yet that was enough to freeze me solid.

I fell hard my freshman year for a classmate named Hal who had a boyish face and grown-up swagger, a love of motorcycles and philosophy, and an inexplicable grin for me. My infatuation drew me into his circle—Scott, Lyle, and Rowland—but abruptly ended when he disappeared one night during exams. His parents came to collect his things and reported that Hal had joined the army. Heartbroken, I shifted my private excitement to a cute if insipid counselor at the Boy Scout camp where I had worked.

First semester sophomore year, I bought a fifth of bourbon with a fake ID and the intention of seducing an ambiguous freshman who ate with us. When I announced at dinner that I had booze, the freshman passed on my invitation, but our friend Marsha accepted. We went back to my dorm and, while *Boris Godunov* highlights played over and over on my portable stereo, I lost my virginity to a woman. Marsha was amused to be my first, the one satisfaction she could take from the evening. I came instantly, three **different** times. The novelty of another naked body was so strong that the gender seemed a minor disappointment.

This was 1971 and we were still waiting for the sixties to reach Virginia. We were all good sons and daughters, although many of us pretended otherwise. Men did not cry, and never touched or embraced each other. Women were expected to be charming. I came from a lower-middle/middle-class family full of Protestant work ethic and Swiss-German chromosomes, the eldest of four kids who were all bound for college despite the expense. I went to school on an ROTC scholarship, a quirk my bookish and bohemian friends politely overlooked. I barely noticed it myself. Coming upon an antiwar protest outside the Campus Center one afternoon, the sidewalk lined with students holding placards, I stopped and chatted with a girl from one of my classes, Ellen, a petite tomboy with long, lank hair and enormous glasses. Neither of us mentioned my combat boots and army fatigues.

Compared to fiction, real life has more characters and incident than necessary. My coming out was a prolonged narrative with a surprising continuity of people. I suspect I write novels instead of short stories because my past is full of such long, tangled strands.

Ellen and her suitemates, Donna and Carolyn, all of them juniors, invited me, Scott, and Lyle, all sophomores, over to their dorm one night for screwdrivers. The women joked about an orgy. In the end, Lyle and Donna passed out on the floor, Scott and Carolyn demurely held hands in a corner, and, on her bed, Ellen and I drunkenly necked and undid clothes and kept going. Afterward, I modestly covered her nudity with mine and we sang "Farewell" with Judy Collins on the radio into each other's ear. "At least you turned off the damn light," Scott grumbled when we left.

Lessening my embarrassment over balling with a friend

among friends was the feeling that I'd proved something: not that I was straight but that I wasn't a disembodied brain after all. I later wondered if Ellen had needed to declare something herself. She was awfully attentive to Donna, who was beautiful. I easily attributed my platonic sexuality to others.

The next time Ellen and I had sex, at the next party, we were sober and withdrew to another room. I confessed, after we finished, that I felt bad because I didn't love her.

"Nothing wrong with good friends having sex now and then," she said.

That seemed reasonable enough. Ellen's flippancy and hiccuplike laugh only half hid a melancholy solitude at her core, but I didn't press the issue, and neither did she.

We went to summer school that year and saw each other regularly, with Scott and Carolyn and Rowland and others, but we were just part of the gang again. The following semester, however, her senior year, Ellen had her own room and we resumed having sex. Our friendship remained on a separate, parallel plane—for me, at least. I remember intimate talks about family in the local deli, but only wary postcoital chats when Ellen lay slim and white on her black velveteen bedspread and I sat naked on her cold floor, both of us wearing our glasses. I liked sex almost as much as I liked being in love, yet was guilty that the two activities did not involve the same person. (Ironically, I can't remember what boy I was in love with that season.) I never spent the night with Ellen, and returned to my dorm feeling oddly sinful, loitered in the lobby, and watched guys who didn't date shoot pool, envying their uncomplicated lives.

There were three or four openly gay men on campus,

but they didn't interest me. More important, I didn't interest them. I knew I gave off the wrong signals, but I refused to remake myself. I wanted to invent my own homosexuality. I wrote a gay short story that year, a chaste account of a high school kid's crush on a college student, more about love and fear than sex. I read it aloud in my writing class, showed it to friends, even published it in our literary magazine. I recognize now what a brash declaration that was, though delivered in a whisper. But nobody heard—not Ellen or that season's infatuatee, only an English professor who didn't mention it until much later, when he said, "I couldn't tell if you were very brave or very stupid."

Ellen and I signed up for a comparative literature seminar with a charismatic teacher notorious for challenging his students' beliefs. In the class were a freckled blur named Sam—I developed a migraine while watching him and found it a most romantic headache—and a transfer student from a Catholic women's college in Wisconsin, a young Italian American named Anna. The teacher enjoyed baiting Anna for being so earnest, but she held her own with him and everyone else.

Ellen and I took a solemn walk in the woods with Scott and Carolyn that spring, on the eve of Ellen's graduation. She was angry with me for talking about new movies when she wanted to talk about . . . she couldn't make clear what she wanted to discuss. I became angry with her anger. We sat against a tree away from the others and looked out on an overcast pond full of stumps and algae.

I went off to ROTC boot camp at Fort Bragg, only to receive a medical discharge from the army for my migraines.

Without the excuse of military service to justify my inaction, I returned to school knowing I should do something about my sexuality. But with whom? I was embedded in straight friends and stamped with the habit of silence. I briefly courted one of my roommates, more in thought than in deed. (One night I desperately lay beside Doug and asked if I could sleep, just sleep, with him. "You're just lonely and drunk," he said nervously.) I buried myself in editing the literary magazine, running the film society, working as a projectionist at the college library, and writing a short novel as an honor's thesis. I lost my temper constantly that year, blind eruptions of anger that had me punching walls and refrigerators and once knocking a plateglass window from a door.

The one bright spot was my new friendship with Anna. I got to know her better when she briefly dated Doug, then on her own. Friends warned her against becoming involved with my circle. We were too moody, they said, too serious, always arguing and hurting each other's feelings, which only intrigued Anna. She had enormous emotional energy—"The girl would wear out a mood ring in a day," someone said—and reported the most startling dreams, such as one where her affectionate father, a veterinarian, took her out to their driveway to put her to sleep with an injection. She was short, bosomy, and very female, but with a wild swing to her arms when she walked. I enjoyed her lack of self-consciousness. She kicked off her shoes to sit in sock feet at the movies. She washed her long black hair with dog shampoo. And I admired her sincerity, the earnestness which some people mistook for innocence but was in fact a fearless desire to address the true and real. She was slowly becoming an ex-Catholic, like Ellen. I decided not to confuse this friendship with sex, and Anna's seriousness guaranteed that wouldn't happen.

I began experimenting with my secret self, telling an acquaintance that I had once been in love with a guy, then telling a friend back home that I'd been in love with *him*. I always spoke in the past tense, as if sharing an amusing anomaly, until one night, over beers, I bluntly told Rowland, "I am gay." A squat, stocky, down-to-earth fellow who constantly pined over women (including my sister), Rowl nodded sympathetically, then asked if it were real or did I just need a new subject for my writing.

2

I FINISHED SCHOOL with no commitments, no notion of what to do next. I stayed on as a projectionist at the college and moved in with Ted, a brainy, competitive extrovert with big teeth, in a complex of old brick apartment buildings outside town. Stuck on Ted, I soon learned that he saw me as solely a live-in ear who could help with the rent. Living downstairs, however, was Hal from freshman year, now back from the army.

I was hurt Hal hadn't searched me out when he returned, but three years was too long to sustain a crush; I'd been in love with an idea before, not an individual. This time I discovered the individual, then slipped him back into the old idea.

The army had changed Hal, although not as much as he thought. It hadn't undone his boyishness. Ted and others called him the Kid. He had been stationed in Germany for two years and so avoided Vietnam. He still had a hard-rubber bounce to his walk and stance, an openness in his spring-loaded smile. With finely turned nose and cheekbones, hair thick and disheveled after years in a GI crew cut, he was carelessly, unconsciously gorgeous. His one flaw, eyes pinched in a permanent squint, only made him seem more human and accessible. I always saw his body whole, never in parts. Dropping by his apartment late one afternoon, I caught a flash of him against a bright window, crossing naked from the shower to his bedroom, a clean silhouette of shoulders, narrow waist, and squared haunches.

We were often together that summer, sometimes with others, frequently alone. When we didn't talk about books or people, we could be companionably silent. Hal strongly identified with Prince Andre from *War and Peace*, a disillusioned stoic, so I became the bumbling, bespectacled Pierre Bezuhov. He clearly enjoyed my company, which seemed promising. And he made no mention of girlfriends or women, which promised more. I anxiously showed him my gay short story. He read it, said he liked its technique, but insisted that the high school kid wasn't gay or even in love, only lonely.

Bored and restless one night, Hal wanted to go to a city and drink. We drove to Norfolk and ended up in a backstreet bar full of Filipino navy stewards who flirted with a brassy, middle-aged Southern belle on crutches. Hal shared his Winstons with me and talked about his stupidity in joining the army, his wasted months in Germany, his inability to decide what to do with his life. He blamed his current misery on his happy childhood. He loved his family very much.

We went out on Granby Street to walk off the beers. Under the empty marquee of a dead movie theater, a man in a gaudy vest asked if we wanted to buy grass. Hal asked if he had any smack. The man said yes, but we had to come back to his place for it. "No, it'll be just me," said Hal.

I was stunned, horrified that Hal could do heroin. And yet, I wanted to go with them and watch Hal shoot up, even do it myself if necessary, for the profane intimacy. He brushed me off as a baby and left with the dealer. Hurt and angry, I waited for him in the grim, half-deserted Greyhound station, worried about how fucked up he'd be when he returned—if he returned.

An hour later, Hal walked in and irritably nodded at me to follow him. There'd been no heroin at the dealer's, only a pal with a knife who told Hal to hand over his money. Hal cursed himself for being suckered. Driving home, he talked about doing smack in the barracks a half-dozen times out of raw boredom. I finally let go with how angry I was, at him for wanting to do that to his body, and myself for wanting to be part of it.

"If you're so damn bored, there's better kicks than heroin."

"Like what?" he said. "Tell me."

But I couldn't. Not yet. Instead I proposed we do something natural and outdoors.

So a week later, Hal and I rented a canoe and went up the Chickahominy River. And it was beautiful: wisps of morning fog curling off the water, crows cawing over the green cornfields, the smooth, glassy river narrowing and widening, chambered like a cow's stomach. Hal's shoulder blades shuttled under his T-shirt while he paddled in the bow and I steered from the stern. We went up a side creek where the trees closed overhead, beached the canoe, sat with our feet in the water, and ate peanut butter and jelly sandwiches. I was sunburned, exhausted, and satisfied, even though we didn't take off our shorts when we went swimming.

Summer ended and I could not move on. I now see that I waited for my buried life to catch up with my college degree. All I really wanted to do was write fiction, but I suffered a failure of confidence, a fear that I didn't know enough to be a writer. Instead I read history, book after book of it, generally about class and revolution. I decided to apply to graduate school in history and remain in Virginia for another year while I supported myself as a night clerk at the local Ramada Inn.

Returning for her senior year at school, Anna was pleased to find me still in town. She and Hal promptly took to each other. Hal had enjoyed our day on the Chickahominy so much that he and his younger sister Ruthie rented a house out there, a half hour from town, a summer cottage with a glassed-in porch, weeping willows, and a pier. He invited me to move in with them. I leaped at the offer, grateful, excited, eternally hopeful.

I lived with Hal and Ruthie that fall and winter, riding into town every day with them (we had only Hal's car and motorcycle) and seeing Anna every night at the library. Free from school, my mind sparked with new ideas and discoveries which I eagerly shared with Anna: Marxism, *Middlemarch*, French New Wave cinema, *The Golden Notebook*. Anna and I were both so intellectually excited that we couldn't always find words for what we wanted to say. We helped each other finish thoughts and sentences, a habit that annoyed our friends when we did it to them.

The Golden Notebook had been recommended by Ellen, who was now in graduate school in Charlottesville. I visited her and we went to bed once more, but on my next trip she said my hot-and-cold attentions confused her and we shouldn't do it again. I sheepishly accepted her terms; the sex confused me, too.

I still couldn't talk about love with Hal. We never talked about sex either. Despite his fondness for alcohol, drugs, and reckless driving, Hal was oddly squeamish, even puritanical, about sex. He preferred classical music. A Eugene Fodor concert excited him into taking up the violin. We drove back to Norfolk with Anna and Ruthie, not to drink but to see *La Bohème.*

My deep longing was diffused and silenced by daily contact with Hal. Frustration slipped out only in odd notes, such as my difficulty in passing a lie detector test required by the motel to work with money, or the party at the house that winter where I got insanely drunk and announced that I wanted to stand naked on our pier in the freezing fire of the stars. Which I did, joined by my friend Bill and a gnomelike philosophy major named Allen. Everyone came out to watch; Ruthie snapped a flash picture. Later at the same party, Anna and I hoisted a very drunk Hal into his bunk and climbed up with him, while other guests wandered in and took turns trying to play his violin.

3

LIFE SEEMED GOOD, until the rainy night I drove Hal's car into a ditch and the insurance company declared it totaled.

Nobody blamed me, but, our transportation gone, we had to move back to town. Hal found a basement room near campus. I returned to my old apartment, where Rowland now lived.

Only then, when we were apart and Hal was no longer a seamless piece of my life, did love kick in as raw, painful need. I felt I had to see Hal at least once a day. I strained to make our time together count. I was working nights, sleeping days. I saw Anna every evening. Often we ate dinner with Hal, who began to do yard work for a retired colonel. I constantly offered to work with him.

I was no longer quietly, unobtrusively present, but actively hunting Hal down.

Suddenly there was tension in the air. Nobody mentioned it, but the mood infected our dreams—and we continued to report dreams to each other. Anna had one where Hal skipped town to reenlist and I was in tears because he didn't say good-bye. Hal dreamed that we three were in a car stopped by a gang of drug dealers and Anna saved us by pulling out a gun we didn't know she had. I dreamed that we galloped in a dangerously small field on three muscular, nearsighted horses without reins. Even Deborah, Anna's roommate, had a nightmare, in which Hal and two other men, neither of them me, beat up Anna and robbed her.

One afternoon at the library, Anna said she needed to talk to me, alone. We went outside. It was beginning to rain, so we went down into the sunken terrace and took shelter under the bridge of the library's entrance. Anna burst into tears and buried her face in my chest. She continued to sob, unable to say anything except "I'm sorry, I'm sorry." The rain fell harder and Anna confessed she couldn't function around people anymore. She didn't know who she was. She didn't feel like a woman when she was with women, she hated the smirkiness of men who treated her as a girl. She enjoyed being with me and Hal, except we made her feel like an intellectual neuter. She could sense affection from us, she said, but nothing physical.

I wanted to explain my sexual indifference, but couldn't. Instead I said that I was bad for her, cold and fucked up. We sank to the pavement while we talked, Anna's hot eyes against my shoulder. She described spending the night with a painter friend, trying this and that with him, without intercourse, and how detached she'd felt. When the rain stopped, Anna got up to leave, saying, "For a cold person you can be very sympathetic."

That night at work, after I balanced the day's accounts, I wrote Hal a letter. I said that I was gay and in love with him and knew it made me demanding, but could he bear with me until it passed. The last clause was not fully sincere. I put the letter in a stamped envelope, but didn't seal it, was not yet ready to send it.

The next afternoon, I found Anna and Hal laughing together in the Campus Center, thoroughly enjoying each other without me.

The day after that, alone with me in the center's cafeteria, Anna talked about how attractive Hal was. "He's so compact. Not just hunky. That, too, but his personality has no loose ends, no frazzles." Then she observed that, whenever Hal and I were together, sparks were thrown off.

"From both of us?" I still couldn't tell.

"Mostly you. Or is that just my imagination?"

I was very excited, very frightened. I reached into my pack, took out the letter, and handed it to her. I knew she was not just a bystander, but involved, in one of two ways.

She read the letter slowly, took a deep breath, and said, "Wow. You're gay? I could feel what you felt about Hal but thought that was only him."

I explained that I'd felt the same about other men, but never women, and never as strongly about anyone as Hal.

Years later, Anna told me that this moment toppled what was left of her Catholicism. "But the Church says homosexuality is immoral," she'd thought. "Except this is Chris and Chris is not immoral, so the Church must be wrong." What she said then was, "I could feel what you felt about Hal. Because I feel the same way myself. About you."

My joy over finally telling the truth to someone who understood became terribly complicated. I was not surprised. It was what I'd feared, although I'd also thought that if Anna loved Hal, things might work out for us all. She could have him if he were straight, I could have him if he were gay, and he'd remain in the family.

"What're we going to do?" I asked.

"I'll go back to Wisconsin. Maybe you'll break through."

We discussed the triangle without anger or alarm, so awed and relieved to be talking that we were not yet distressed by an impossible situation. Despite her own stake, Anna did not dismiss Hal as a lost cause for me. She was as mystified as I was by the bend of his heart.

Then Hal strolled into the cafeteria, grinning and shining after an afternoon of yard work. With his army fatigue pants, pink tie-dyed T-shirt, and the cockeyed stance that turned his entire body into a friendly smirk, he was both less and more real than the figure Anna and I had discussed. He seemed pleased to see us together. We went to a nearby diner for dinner, where we were joined by Allen, the philosophy gnome.

I hated being around Allen. At the end of the month, after exams, Hal was driving a family car cross-country to leave it with his older brother in California. He'd told me he needed to take the trip alone, but Allen had invited himself along as far as Denver. I wasn't jealous. Allen was a clown, socially awkward and nuttily abstract. Hal clearly pitied him. I feared that he had only pity for me as well.

Over the next days I kept forgetting and remembering to show Anna the consideration I hoped Hal would show me. Early one evening, the three of us went for a walk in the woods around the campus lake. We came to a rope swing and Hal had to give it a try, gracefully sailing over the pollen-speckled water and back. Trying to follow his example, I slipped and fell in. We all ended up in the cold lake, laughing and splashing in our clothes. Hal went to his nearby basement to change. My apartment was on the other side of town, so I accepted Anna's suggestion that I use the dryer in her dorm.

I sat in her room, wrapped in a bedspread like a chenille toga, chatting with Anna and Deborah about a book by George Steiner while we waited for my clothes to dry. With an unexpectedly nasty smile, Anna dared me to give them a show. I accepted the dare, but found that the thought of nudity gave me an erection. Not wanting her to misunderstand, I exposed myself only in sections. Then Anna asked her roommate to leave, there was something she needed to tell me.

She was still depressed, she said. She talked about the men she'd loved and how emotional she became in their presence, wondering *at* them so much it hurt. She began to cry. I sat beside her in my bedspread, her hood of black hair against my bare shoulder. And despite everything I knew, I kissed her. I hoped she would refuse my body, knowing where I was coming from. Instead, she asked me to turn off the light and undressed slowly, worriedly.

I told myself this wasn't real sex—we used only our hands and my mouth—but I couldn't pretend we were just friends fooling around. Our two naked bodies seemed only large and awkward to me without undivided lust to draw them taut. My mind was split from my body, full of fear and responsibility. And yes, there was the stupid hope that if I were kind to Anna, then Hal would be kind to me. As if the categorical imperative works in sex, as if sex were going to solve this—although with superficial longing, sometimes an orgasm is all that's needed.

When we finished, I asked Anna if it'd helped or been irrelevant, as if her depression weren't about me. She said it had helped some, but she didn't want me to feel obligated to do it again.

Strangely enough, it did seem to help. Anna went out a few nights later with her painter. I went off with Hal, Allen, and Rowland to share several pitchers of beer at the deli and cheerfully argue about the nonexistence of God and the human need for transcendence. "But when you're dead, you're dead," said Rowland. We rode home together in his car, dropping off Allen, then Hal. Bold and tipsy, and challenged by my night with Anna, I reached into my pack and gave Hal the letter I still carried. "I wanted you to see this. Good night."

Back home, Rowland heated a can of spaghetti and discussed his chances with my sister while I worried that Hal would never speak to me again. Someone knocked at our door. It was Hal. He looked serious. He said he couldn't sleep and had gone for a walk—three miles to our apartment. He asked if I'd like to join him.

We marched up the long, dark highway toward Frank's Truck Stop without speaking, cicadas chattering in the kudzu along the shoulders, my nerves strung between terror and hope.

Hal launched into the story of a girl from four years ago, now married, who had been his real reason for joining the army. He'd chosen flight over responsibility, he said. He talked about his history with women, how he'd had sex twice, in brothels in Germany. "Because of this feeling about women," he said, as if he'd made that feeling clear, "all my close relations are with men. I consider you one of my closest friends."

Then he chastised himself for lying, always lying, although the lies he cited were trivial, such as his tale of losing a hundred dollars in a crap game. This led to an existential turn, talk about the lie of meaning, the lie of God. "Prince Andre is a lie," he sneered. "All is a lie over a void of despair." He respected Allen yet scorned his belief that greater meaning existed if only he could find it. Hal believed the universe was meaningless. He wished Allen weren't coming on his drive west; he wanted to be alone and authentic.

I tried to insert myself into this metaphysical murk by saying that I didn't care about greater meaning, only the tick-tock of my own emotions. "Which I guess makes me a lesser person than you or Allen," I bitterly added.

"Or greater," said Hal, without conviction. "Maybe greater."

We were at the Truck Stop now, eating eggs and grits. Impatiently waiting for him to get to us, I suddenly wondered if he'd misread my letter and missed the part about my being in love with him. So I followed his airy monologue with a detailed story of my infatuation, from freshman year through our months on the Chickahominy River. I ended by saying that, of the men I'd loved, he was the only one who deserved admiration.

He listened without comment, only discomfort, then skated off into fresh abstractions.

On the hike back, I claimed to have a low threshold of need. All I required to requite my love was his friendship.

"That you have," he said. "That you have."

When we reached my building, I invited him in, but he insisted he needed to walk some more and forget the stupid things he had said. We embraced—me with both arms, Hal with one. I stood alone and watched him wane in and out of streetlight halos until he was gone. I was thoroughly baffled, touched by his coming to talk, disappointed by how little he'd had to say. He seemed to have said no, but so abstractly that I wasn't sure what to think. Neither of us had mentioned sex.

When I told Anna about it the next day, she sympathized with Hal: learning a friend was gay must be a shock for someone who knew homosexuality only by hearsay, a complete rupture of meaning, which was why he'd turned existential. I could not believe Hal was so ignorant; I wondered if his philosophical smoke hid something else.

Exams began, adding to the stress. I waited for Hal to continue our conversation, but he didn't. He remained himself when we were with others, but avoided being alone with me. One evening among a pack of friends, he grumbled that "a queer" had tried to pick him up the night before. I was stung but said nothing. That weekend the pack went on a picnic and Hal offered to put suntan lotion on my back. I sat very still while his large, callused hands rubbed my skin. I glanced over at Anna, who was as surprised by the gesture as I was.

Anna and I were thrown closer together. Because Hal wouldn't discuss it, she became my partner for talk of my love, just as I was her only confidant for her love of me.

Alone at the Ramada one night, sitting behind the front desk at four o'clock, the hour of the wolf, I fell into a cold, deep rage. I imagined using a shotgun on anyone who'd ever caused me grief—first an old roommate whose journal I'd once read, then a teacher who'd snubbed me, then Hal, and finally Anna. I wanted to horrify myself, but the images had an oddly soothing effect.

A week remained before Hal would leave for the summer and Anna forever. She was starting graduate school in Wisconsin. The three of us spent an evening together, walking around town, Anna saying good-bye to people. Hal seemed at ease with me again. I was working with him for the colonel the next day. Anna appeared cheerful, until she abruptly drew me aside and whispered, "I can't spend tonight alone. Please." I promised to come to her room later, after I walked out to my apartment and got my bike, which I needed to ride to the colonel's in the morning. Hal and I told her good night and resumed walking.

"Odd how reluctant everyone is to part tonight," he said wistfully.

"Yeah, well," I muttered. "I'm the apex of a crazy triangle." I hadn't said a word to him about Anna and me.

"Yeah. I know." He smiled. "Except there's no geometry in life. Only in mathematics."

"Do I make you uncomfortable?"

"No! What makes you say a stupid thing like that? I feel more comfortable around you than with anyone. Outside my family."

That pleased me. Yet after we said good night, I felt cowardly for not pressing harder. I wanted Hal to be as agitated and confused as I was.

Bicycling back to town on my way to Anna's dorm, I stopped by Hal's basement. His light was off. I assumed he was still out walking. Intending to wait up for him, I went into his room (we never locked our doors) and turned on the light.

He was on the bed, startled awake after falling asleep. He still wore his fatigue pants—as if afraid I might drop by.

I apologized for waking him, but he invited me to stay. He got up and put water on for tea.

"What're you doing here?" he finally asked. "Weren't you going to go to—?" He couldn't finish, did not want to admit he'd overheard Anna and me set our rendezvous. I read disapproval in his silence. He did not want me to spend the night with Anna?

"Where am I sleeping tonight?" I said. "You tell me. I have two choices, don't I?"

He made a face and looked away.

"I'd go to bed with you at the drop of a hat, Hal. But it has to be your hat."

I wanted him to drop his hat, out of affection or jealousy or even to protect Anna. But once I made clear that my love of him was sexual, my insistence softened, my sympathy with his unease returned. I asked if he knew his brother's address in California, so I could write.

"No!"

He didn't want another letter. While we drank our tea, he took up a book of stories by Albert Camus and read aloud about a man who has his tongue cut out. I thought he was asking me to shut up. I finished my tea and said I'd see him the next day.

Not until a week later, after Hal left town, did I wonder if he'd read me the Camus to confess that he couldn't give tongue to something he wanted to say. Silent myself for so long, I thought I understood. I know now, years after the fact, that what Hal wanted to tell me was not what I wanted to hear. Anna's guess was closer to the truth: Hal was more old-fashioned than I'd ever imagined. He found homosexuality not just alien but unnatural, even evil. I was his first gay man, just as I was Anna's, inept though I was. I spoiled his moral certainty, yet Hal liked and respected me and remained loyal, despite his confusion.

I arrived at Anna's dorm at three in the morning. She apologized, said it wasn't fair when the beloved was also the confidant. She was angry with herself for needing me, angry with me for giving in. My mood was as foul as hers. We spent the night together, just sleeping, both of us in underpants. Her muscles formed a deep cup in the small of her back.

The next day Hal and I went out to the colonel's and worked together, lugging flagstones for a walkway, as though nothing dangerous had been touched on the previous night.

Anna's family came to town for her graduation, and she was no longer free for late-night confidences.

They departed within hours of each other. Hal left in the afternoon, taking me and Anna out to the Truck Stop to say good-bye to us together. Anna and I wasted our last night by riding to Newport News with Rowland and friends to see *Mandingo*, stopping off afterward at an all-night supermarket with a restaurant for coffee. Needing to be alone, Anna and I went for one last walk, not in the woods or on a dark street this time, but in the produce section of the Giant Open Air Market. She asked for an update of my last days with Hal. I had nothing to report. "If only he were interested in women," I said. "Then I'd have no reason to hope." I confessed how, seeing her with Hal, I wanted them to become a couple and set me free. Anna said she'd had a dream where she and Hal made love while I watched in disgust, and another dream where she made love to a woman and I was nowhere around. We rode back to town holding hands. Anna spent that night with her parents at their motel before she left with them the next morning. We promised each other we'd write.

I woke up the next day bereft yet relieved that both legs of my triangle were gone, much as Jules feels at the end of *Jules and Jim*, when his wife and his best friend are dead.

4

THIS WAS MERELY the end of the beginning, just as coming out is only a beginning. Doors were unlocked; none had been opened. We were like a piece of chamber music where a single theme is tried by one instrument, then another and the next, in every key and variation until all is resolved in a completed phrase or silence.

I saw Ellen again shortly after that day of good-byes in 1975, visiting her in Washington before she left for Europe to see Scott and Carolyn, now married and living in Edinburgh. I'd written her about Hal. She wrote back, "Now I get it. I never understood what you wanted from me, but you needed a disguise."

The letter infuriated me. Going with her when she picked up her passport and tickets, I argued with her letter. Yes, I'd been mute and selfish, I admitted, but had never pretended we were more in public than what we'd been in private. And I never lied about my lack of feeling, quoting back her line, "What's wrong with friends having sex now and then?" She admitted her own careless indecision over me, and more recent problems with love and sex, men and women. She criticized me, however, for confusing someone like Anna. I pleaded guilty.

Six months later, still in the same Virginia town but with my own apartment, I finally got one male, then another, into bed. It was easier than I'd imagined, although both were only curious, timid, and drunk. (One of them threw up before sex, the other threw up after.) Getting to Europe myself that fall, I was set to spend the night in the train station in Amsterdam when a passing Dutchman who looked like a truck driver said I could sleep at his place. I followed him home, still unsure what this laconic Good Samaritan had in mind when we casually undressed on either side of his only bed. He idly slipped off his peach-colored briefs just as he turned out the light, so I shed my skivvies and climbed in, wondering if the Dutch simply slept in the nude. We instantly seized each other, and I found that sex with any man who wanted me as frankly as I wanted him, even a stranger, engaged my body to its depths in ways that sex with women never had.

When I returned to Virginia, Hal asked me to move in with him again. It suggested a promising change of attitude, but while I was gone, Hal's search for meaning had ended in a leap of religious faith. Anna had been in town for the disturbing privilege of seeing him jump into beliefs that she'd jumped out of. Hal's Christianity was not fundamentalist or narrow, but tentative, open, even existential. It did not stop me from falling in love with him again. It did not turn Hal against me when I told him how I still felt. He asked only that I respect his wishes. I sighed as lover but obeyed as a friend, and occasionally spent the night with an acquaintance who was in love with *his* straight roommate, a six-foot-six exterminator.

Not until Hal finally began to date women, a year later, did I abandon all hope of love. He was quite straight, yet as slow in coming to terms with his desires as I'd been with mine. Heterosexuality is not always as easy as it looks. I do not presume to understand, but it was as if Hal needed to shore up the uncertainty of self with something larger—religion, meaning, God—before he could expose it in love and intimacy.

Anna and I remained in touch, writing and visiting each other in different cities. Distance kept the resentment and guilt of unrequited love out of all that was good in our bond, usually.

Hal started med school. I moved to New York, ostensibly for the urban experience I needed as a writer. I found more basic, physical and emotional experience instead. Anna came to the city to take a graduate course at Columbia that summer, then stayed on. I was overjoyed to be with her again. Very slowly, however, it resumed, our schizophrenia of angry love and necessary friendship, and it was worse than before. We were not so timid about what we craved and required. If either of us had been more sensible, or more cowardly, we would've broken off completely. I still cannot think about one period without feeling ill over the pain we inflicted on each other.

The fights did not end until Anna left for Buffalo to resume graduate school. Ellen had transferred there and reported tons of ready fellowship money. She needed a roommate. She and Anna knew each other more by reputation than time spent together, but they assumed they could get along.

That was in August 1979. Two months later in a bar, I met an art director from Tennessee who loved movies as much as I did. We saw each other every other night for weeks, then months, without running out of talk or shared interests or warmth. Requited love was a new world for me, a strange, baffling peace. The morning of my twenty-seventh birthday, Draper asked me to move in with him.

Anna and I remained in touch. Again, distance helped. She telephoned one night that spring, sounding oddly content, even tickled. She quickly told me why.

"I'm in love."

"Who is he?"

"It's she," said Anna in a very small voice. "It's Ellen. And she loves me."

I was thrown by the symmetry—fiction could never get away with anything so neat—and said, "But you're so different."

She laughed. "I'm afraid we're too much alike."

I was also thinking: Of course. They belong together.

I later came up with the image of Ellen as rock and Anna as fire, which does justice to neither but suggests how they complete each other. When Draper and I visited Buffalo that fall, I saw that they were goofily in love, but also that Anna brought Ellen out of her solitude and melancholy, while Ellen smoothed and anchored Anna's wild swings of mood. They had far more in common than their detour through me. (Anna recently confessed how, in the seminar where we first met, she'd been equally struck by me and Ellen, attracted physically and mentally to us both yet certain neither of us would ever notice her existence.)

Perhaps we were only symptoms of one another's homosexuality, but the three of us seem to have shared something more valuable than error. I like to think it was a belief that the conflicting jumbles of emotion, intellect, sex, and—there's no other phrase for it—moral life actually do connect and can be experienced most fully by two bodies speaking to and through each other. This reckless ideal appealed to us all, even Hal, but Anna pursued it furthest, without fear or compromise. In her friendship with me, she found herself in a house with too many sealed rooms. Then she met Ellen, whose rooms were all open to her.

That July, Hal married Becky, a smart, attractive, subtly tough woman who later became a pediatrician. Anna was unable to go south for the wedding, but I attended and gave her a detailed report the next time we spoke. Hal and Becky spent the following summer in Honduras as rural medics.

They have three kids now, but are no longer in Virginia, so I don't see them. Hal remains full of passionate beliefs, some I agree with, some I don't. His Catholicism is more doctrinaire than his wife's, but my loyalty to him has made me more open-minded about religion than is natural to my skepticism. Hal might be described as liberal-leftist in his politics and ultraconservative in his moral attitudes, with one glaring exception.

Not long before they moved, I went down for a visit. Hal and I were exiled to the porch one evening so I could smoke (Hal had quit). We discussed a mutual friend, a so-called confirmed bachelor who actually lives the life of a confirmed bachelor. I'd never shared my suspicions about Mitch. Suddenly, without prompting from me, Hal snapped in exasperation, "Why can't Mitch wake up and accept that he's gay? He needs to go out and meet guys. It's the one way he's ever going to be happy."

We continue to confuse each other into more complicated, less easy, truer understandings.

1996

LITTLE GREEN
BUDDIES

—⁓—

I T IS OFTEN noted that literature contains
few full-blooded portrayals of real friendship. What is even stranger is the rarity of
such portrayals in children's books. After all,
books about adults are usually about adultery,
a subject children's books tend to avoid. You
might expect the empty space to be filled by
the subject of friendship, but no, the great
majority of children's books are about lone
individuals dealing with the obstacles of the
world. The obstacles can come in the guise
of a fire-breathing dragon, a logic-chopping

caterpillar, an anarchistic cat in a beat-up top hat, Farmer McGregor, a stony stepmother, or the protagonist's own stupidity. Occasionally the protagonist is given company, maybe a sibling or a pet, but the company is there only to provide a spectator or an additional obstacle. Even when the stories are closer to home and take place in the real world of backyards and classrooms, friends only take the form of a gang, a heartless, poly-faced Hindu god that usually goes by a name like Samandjimmyandanna. The one-on-one friendship that is the source of so many pleasures and aggravations in childhood is bizarrely absent in children's books. It was this absence that must have been noticed ten years ago when writer and illustrator Arthur Lobel began a series of stories for beginning readers about the adventures of two friends. To the limited company of great fictional friendships—Don Quixote and Sancho Panza, Huck and Jim, Bouvard and Pecuchet, Jules and Jim—Lobel added the names of Frog and Toad.

Frog and Toad are, as their names suggest, a frog and a toad. Frog is green, tall, usually dressed in striped trousers and a brown sports coat without a collar. Toad is brown, shorter, and wears a green plaid jacket with green trousers. Neither wears shoes. Their world is an odd mix of the anthropomorphic and the natural, the childlike and the adult. They live in tiny Tudor cottages that are surrounded by immense stalks of grass and flowers as big as suns. They are financially independent bachelors who are given to drinking copious amounts of tea, and yet have the emotions of two very perceptive six-year-olds. It is the world of *The Wind in the Willows*, only scaled down for a younger reader, and if there is a precedent for

Lobel's work here, it is in Kenneth Grahame's chapters about the friendship of Mole and Water Rat.

In themselves, the Frog and Toad stories are not cause for wonder. Published in four books that began with *Frog and Toad Are Friends* in 1970, they are cleanly written, well illustrated, occasionally achieving a snap that even an adult can enjoy, but with nothing that really lifts them above the better tradition of imaginative beginner books that includes the work of Maurice Sendak, some Dr. Seuss, James Marshall, and other books by Lobel himself. But in the context of children's literature, the focus of the Frog and Toad stories is new and even quietly exciting. For here the source of interest is not the friends' adventures, most of which are trivial even by the standards of the most undemanding child, but the give and take of their friendship. Not even Kenneth Grahame makes the reader so concious of the work involved in friendship, or of the pleasures that make that work worth the effort.

Most of that work is the result of the different natures of the two friends. Toad is somewhat neurotic. He worries constantly, loiters in bed (five of the twenty stories begin with Toad, like Oblomov, swaddled in bedclothes) and tends toward obsessive-compulsive behavior, such as making a list of the things he must do that day (Wake up, Get dressed, Eat breakfast, Visit Frog—a very simple lifestyle, even for an animal). Frog, on the other hand, is sanely healthy. He likes sports, gardening, and telling stories. He is occasionally insensitive to Toad's wants. In the movie, Toad would be played by Woody Allen, Frog by Gerard Depardieu. It is an uneven relationship, with Toad often playing the younger brother to Frog, and there is the feeling that he needs Frog more than Frog needs him. But the deck isn't stacked so that either the reader or Frog feels smug toward Toad. On more than one occasion, Frog's common sense comes out second best to Toad's neurotic instincts.

Lobel plays down the didactic intent by filling out the books with episodes that do not bring friendship to trial: Frog and Toad eat cookies, Frog and Toad fly a kite, or go sledding or rake leaves. They do things together, do them differently, and their friendship serves only as a backdrop. But it is when Lobel is at his most didactic and brings friendship to the center, usually in only one story per book, that the tales really catch fire.

Such a story is "The Dream" from *Frog and Toad Together*, in which Toad dreams that he is performing in an enormous theater with only Frog for an audience. "PRESENTING THE GREATEST TOAD IN ALL THE WORLD!" announces a distant voice, and Toad proudly plays the piano, walks a tightrope, and dances. Each act is applauded by Frog, who confesses that he can do none of those things. And as he applauds, Frog becomes smaller and smaller and smaller, until he disappears. Toad sees what he's done, breaks out of his narcissism, cries out for Frog, and begins to spin in the empty darkness. Suddenly, Toad wakes up and finds Frog standing beside his bed. Toad is overjoyed to find his friend back to his usual size, once again the same, big contented lug, standing in the bedroom with one hand in a pocket.

"Frog," he said,
"I am so glad
you came over."
"I always do," said Frog.

And the two go outside and spend the day playing together. The story is amazing not only because it opens a can of worms—the dream is weighted with Toad's resentment of always being the inferior—but because it promptly throws the worms away. Questions of who is better or smarter or stronger only threaten a friendship and have nothing to do with its pleasures. The pleasures are obvious in Toad's joy and Frog's quietly loyal, "I always do." No psychoanalyst ever discarded the worms more deftly.

In the same vein is "Alone," the last story in *Days with Frog and Toad*. Toad finds a note on Frog's door saying that he has gone off to be alone. Toad is disturbed by the note, hunts for Frog, and finally sees him on a rock in the middle of the river. Deciding that his friend needs to be cheered up, Toad fixes a lunch of sandwiches and iced tea and gets a turtle to take him out to the rock. The turtle, one of those obnoxious creatures who agrees with everything you say, echoes Toad's fears that maybe Frog *wants* to be alone, and even that Frog doesn't want to be Toad's friend anymore. Stirred into a fit of anxiety, Toad falls off the turtle and into the river. Frog pulls Toad and the lunch basket onto the rock and consoles Toad for the ruined lunch that was meant to make him happy.

"But Toad," said Frog.
"I *am* happy. I am very happy.
This morning
when I woke up
I felt good because
the sun was shining.

I felt good because
I was a frog."

And, of course, he felt good because he had Toad for a friend.

"Now," said Frog,
"I will be glad *not* to be alone.
Let's eat lunch."
Frog and Toad
stayed on the island
all afternoon.
They ate wet sandwiches
without iced tea.
They were two close friends
sitting alone together.

What I would give to have written that last sentence.

By now, you are probably wondering, both because of this review and the nature of the magazine you are reading, if Frog and Toad might just possibly be, well, gay. True, they do not sleep together or even share the same house, but the intensity of their attentions and worries certainly point in a homosexual direction. I do not really need that possibility. The scope of the stories seems so much broader. Although Frog and Toad are more consistently loyal and kind than the children I remember or know, the fervor of their relationship rings true for all childhood friendships. Such friendships are our first opportunity to connect with someone to whom we are not bound by authority or physical need. They don't always make up in intensity for what they lack in duration, but perhaps they serve as half-forgotten models for our relationships with people when we grow older, whether as friends, spouses, or lovers.

Lobel chose to take these original contacts seriously. And he chose to make those contacting creatures male. Simply by changing pronouns, he could have made his friends female, or one female and the other male. Society expects its females to be sharply conscious of each move in the intricate business of friendship, but expects its males, even as children, to be above such attention to emotional detail. By making both of his friends members of the "strong" gender, Lobel goes against convention. He never draws attention to this revolt. Lobel presents his amphibians' attention to details as something natural and unbounded by gender, which it is. Not only do Frog and Toad live in a fulfilled dream of loyalty and kindness, they live in a world that approaches a true sexual democracy.

1981

HEARTS OF STONE:
AIDS AND THE COMMON READER

—w—

WHY READ FICTION about AIDS? There are more efficient ways of getting the terrible news. People who already live with the epidemic rarely want to relive it in their imaginations. Most people who live without AIDS, or the grief or confusion of AIDS, don't want to think about it at all. Even those who write the books make nervous jokes about BWAs—books with AIDS.

And yet, the books continue to be written and, more surprisingly, read. The literary response to the epidemic has been extraordinary, its quantity matched by strength, scope, and quality. Michael Denneny, Michael Bronski, and others have written well on the cultural and political importance of this literature. I want to explore why AIDS fiction is valuable and even necessary to the common reader.

In many ways it's easier to understand why this fiction is written than why people read it. Writers write out of their own raw feelings, to house pain and confusion, however briefly, in a separate structure of words. I felt the need to write about AIDS long before I began my own novel, *In Memory of Angel Clare*. I was relatively unscathed, yet I had my demons and uncertainties, and the epidemic was the most important thing happening in my world. I had to wait until I found a story, a bit of armor that allowed me to draw closer to guilts and fears I could not deal with alone, including my own uneasy privilege of health. I found it in the conflict between a young widower and his dead lover's friends. I cheated, going at AIDS from a slant, but maybe all art is an attempt to cheat circumstance.

What kind of stories can one tell about AIDS? Medicine continues to dictate a single brutal plot: You get sick and die. You might live for several months or several years, but you eventually die. You often die young. Society can add another twist in that you die stigmatized, an outcast. What can an author do with that except rework the death of Little Nell? The wasting away of a fourteen-year-old girl from a nameless Victorian illness was the climax of *The Old Curiosity Shop* by Charles Dickens, melting its original readers, high and low, in a warm wash of tears. Their response only puzzles or embarrasses us today.

"One must have a heart of stone to read the death of Little Nell without laughing," Oscar Wilde famously quipped—while he was free on bail and awaiting the trial that would send him to prison; Wilde was in a good position to see the absurdity of pity for pity's sake.

There has been no death of Little Nell in AIDS fiction. The pathos of the situation is so strong, one can't help feeling Nell's presence in the wings, but every book I've read works hard to keep her out. Even in novels that do slip into pathos, the author can be felt straining to avoid conventional tears. This rejection of the sentimental obvious is due partly to contemporary taste: we distrust least emotions that lie too deep for tears. But it also comes from our recognition that tears come too easily here and cannot be ends in themselves. Very few readers can have a good cry over a death in an AIDS novel, close the book, and feel finished with the subject; certainly no gay man can.

What can an author give and a reader take besides tears? Thinking back on what I've read and seen over the past five years, I find several valid approaches writers use to get us beyond the death of Little Nell. Call them narrative strategies or points of focus, each is grounded in a simple moral observation.

AIDS has a personal reality. The most obvious yet necessary thing AIDS fiction can do is calmly tell us what an individual experiences when he or she becomes ill. Meaning as well as tears are withheld: this is what happened; this is what they felt. Often the character is still alive at the end of the story, not so much an act of kindness to the reader as a way to avoid pathos and the feeling of closure death would give. These stories extract a personal life from the public sensationalism of headlines, statistics, and blame. Sensationalism here means presenting a situation as so bleak and devastating, that one can't imagine living with it on a daily basis. But to describe something as unimaginable is to make an excuse for refusing to think about it at all.

Some of the best examples came early in the epidemic. William Hoffman's play *As Is* gave AIDS a human face for many whose only experience was limited to rumor and the media. Several more recent works seem written, in part, as correctives to the public imagery of TV and newspaper coverage. *Valley of the Shadow* by Christopher Davis ends not with a deathbed scene but a brief obituary identical to those printed regularly in the gay press; the novel itself recovers one of the ordinary lives hidden by those perfunctory paragraphs. *At Risk* by Alice Hoffman is clearly inspired by the case of Ryan White, the young hemophiliac whose persecution drew attention because he was "an innocent victim" (the press still loves Little Nell even if fiction doesn't); Hoffman imagines the family life hidden under the media coverage.

This contrast between public perception and personal reality is overtly used in "The *Times* as It Knows Us" by Allen Barnett in *The Body and Its Dangers* to shape an incisive account of a weekend in a houseful of gay men on Fire Island. One of the men has AIDS and one ARC, three are HIV-positive, and all have suffered the loss of friends or lovers. There's a crisis when one comes down with a fever. Some of the men behave badly, others admirably; everyone has his reasons. Framing it all, almost looking on, is the fatuous presence of the *New York Times*, represented by the AIDS articles and editorials obsessively clipped by the narrator, a history of glib commentary and fake omniscience—the media as paper god.

The personal can also be painfully private. *Bloodstream* by Joel Redon stays very close to the daily thoughts and experiences of Peter, a PWA who returns from New York to his family in Oregon. There are visits to a therapy group in a nearby city and a tentative friendship with another PWA, but the novel concentrates on Peter's life alone with his family. Redon's prose is quietly restrained, without being evasive, as he follows Peter from remission to relapse to remission again. The awful solitude of illness comes through without self-pity. The temptation of pity is mocked by the needs of Peter's father, a failed businessman whose hunger for sympathy puts him in competition with his son. AIDS does not purge people's differences and drive them together; it heightens what already existed without changing the fundamentals.

Life goes on even during an epidemic. There are novels where AIDS is present without being at the center; it's just there, an adamant fact of history. This is how the fortunate majority, gay as well as straight, continues to experience the epidemic. Fiction should explore the ways AIDS does and doesn't affect those outside the storm.

At one end of the scale is silence, but the presence of AIDS is so strong silence can read very loud to a contemporary reader. It can even reach back to color our reading of books written before the epidemic. Two novels as different as *Faggots* by Larry Kramer and *Dancer from the Dance* by Andrew Holleran now seem to be specifically about life before AIDS, Kramer's a savage jeremiad, Holleran's a romantic elegy.

Recent novels address AIDS in detail without letting it take over the foreground. *Mountain Climbing in Sheridan Square* by Stan Leventhal includes episodes about the illness and death of friends. The book is constructed in discrete episodes, snapshots of one gay man's life shuffled together without chronology, a method that enables Leventhal to deal with AIDS without giving it more importance than he gives other aspects of his narrator's life. It's a fictional equivalent of the way many gay men remain sane in the face of the epidemic, a compartmentalization with unlocked doors between the compartments. *Horse Crazy* by Gary Indiana, on the other hand, shows how the epidemic can cause insane behavior. Restricted to the narrator's visits to a friend in the hospital, AIDS is kept in the background of a story of an unrequited obsession for a handsome ex-junkie, a background already thick with anxiety. The reader can't help feeling that AIDS dread is responsible for the narrator's masochistic choice of a love object, the pain of a heart rubbed raw a distraction from his feelings of malaise and helplessness.

Then there are the stories set in the aftermath of death. The moment of high drama and pathos is over, but other lives go on. My own novel can be mentioned here, along with *Afterlife* by Paul Monette, which follows the friendship of three AIDS widowers, and Edmund White's short story, "An Oracle," from *The Darker Proof*, where an American in Crete remembers life with his deceased lover while imagining he's found love again with a young Greek. These works examine the loose ends left by any death, the ritual of mourning and what it enables us to feel or not feel. But, in the context of AIDS, grief is only the eye of a storm that has not yet passed.

Comedy can be a means of control as well as denial. Almost all AIDS fiction uses humor in one form or another, if only in black jokes made by people in pain. If pathos simplifies mixed feelings to tears, comedy acknowledges the contradictions and uses their absurdity to cool down emotions. If an author or character has enough control of pain to see the comedy present, then we can approach them less afraid of being overwhelmed by bathos, self-pity, or bad writing.

Comic seriousness works best when the pain is clearly visible, neither buried nor magnified by jokes. The strongest example of this is the Adam Mars-Jones short story "Slim," also from *The Darker Proof,* where a middle-aged, English PWA describes the mental strategies he uses to deal with illness. It's all in his voice, a wit like the steel frame of what was once a flamboyant sense of humor. He calls AIDS "slim," an African name for the disease, and mocks his healthcare giver by referring to the man simply as Buddy:

> Buddy's very good. That sounds suitably grudging. He tries to fit in with me. He doesn't flinch if I talk about my chances of making Slimmer of the Year. He's learned to say *black currants.* He said "lesions" just the once, but I told him it wasn't a very vivid use of the language, and if he wasn't a doctor he had no business with it.

There's nothing here to make one laugh out loud, yet it is comedy, a heroic kind of irony. One man continues to exercise wit in the presence of real pain, without ever denying that pain.

Comedy is slippery, of course. What registers as humorous

with one reader might seem callous to another or not regis-
ter at all with a third. Look at the different responses to *Eighty-
Sixed* by David B. Feinberg. The novel is a series of stand-up riffs
by the narrator, B.J. Rosenthal, about his life as a gay man in
New York City—the first half about the vicissitudes of sleeping
around in search of a boyfriend in 1980, the second half about
fear and trembling during the epidemic in 1986. No emotion
is confessed without the padded glove of a joke, wisecracks
with the desperate patter of someone straining to keep his feelings under control. B.J. himself understands exactly what he's
doing, but can't break out of it. A problem with the book is that
all the characters, not just B.J., hide inside the same mechanical
one-liners, some of them quite vicious. As a result, the characters blur together, a world made anonymous by panic—or
the author's method. The jokes paint an all-consuming anxiety without ever unpacking and examining its personal parts.
The comedy not only represses pathos, it magnifies it, so when
B.J. finally breaks through to tears over the death of a former
trick—tears skipped over and referred back to, the elliptical
way sex scenes were once handled in fiction—the novel seems
like a return to Little Nell by postmodern means.

Eighty-Sixed has its enemies—readers who find it callous and
unfunny or glibly defeatist—but the book has many admirers,
too, who must find its black-and-white extremes of smart jokes
and elliptical tears a good way to think about AIDS without
being overwhelmed.

Fantasy is an escape, but one that offers a view from outside.
Trapped in reality, which with AIDS means death, the writer
paints a door on the wall of his cell and pretends we can walk

through it. Magic realism comes from the need to escape the limits of conventional reality. The harsher the reality, the stronger the need to escape. Without reality to drive or ground it, fantasy is only whimsy.

Concentrating first on the sheer reality of AIDS, fiction is just now exploring the alternatives. Nevertheless, one of the most interesting experiments came early on in *Second Son* by Robert Ferro. In the midst of a realistic novel about two lovers with AIDS, there's a subplot about a cult of gay men who believe aliens will take them to the safety of another planet. The cult is first mentioned jokingly in a letter from a friend, a bit of satire about the New Age nostrums that spring up around the epidemic. Later letters describe the cult in more detail, until the friend reports he's joined them in the desert, where they watch the skies and beam radio signals into space, a community of hope and waiting.

As slippery as comedy, fantasy elicits different responses from different readers. Many dismiss this aspect of *Second Son* as escapist nonsense. But the space cult can also be treated as an expression of longing, nothing more, a metaphor of the desire for a cure or solution, fragile yet touching in its silliness. I wish Ferro had gone even further and sent the two lovers out to join their friend in the desert. But only if the aliens did not come. The arrival of a spaceship would take the fantasy out of the realm of dream and metaphor, where it has psychological validity, into the commonplace of formula science fiction.

Fantasy can be as expressive as dreams are, when we know the facts of the life outside the dream. Fantasy is often presented through dreams in AIDS fiction, imagination domesticated for realist use. *The Irreversible Decline of Eddie Socket* by John Weir uses a wildly baroque dream about crucifixion at Rockefeller Plaza to dramatize a young PWA's self-destructive mix of Catholic guilt and theatrical self-pity.

Or fantasy can begin in the dreams of realistic characters and go on to take over a work completely, as happens in Tony Kushner's six-hour play, *Angels in America.* In the opening scenes, we're introduced to a broad spectrum of very real people: a gay WASP with AIDS, his leftist Jewish lover, the lover's repressed Mormon boss, the boss's pill-addicted wife, and Roy Cohn. The wife hallucinates visits to the Antarctic; the PWA dreams encounters with his ancestors. His dreams become the play's reality when an angel, like a figure in a Renaissance painting, brings him a message he must pass on to the world. Fantasy is presented in the guise of comedy, but anchoring it all, keeping the play from floating off in its own ingenuity, is the attention paid to social realities and people's motives. Even Cohn is given good arguments for what he does, rationalizations that would seem plausible to him if to nobody else. After Cohn is diagnosed with AIDS, he too crosses into the dream reality and is visited by the ghost of Ethel Rosenberg. What begins as one man's escape from illness into fantasy becomes a meditation on American history, politics, and religion.

Frustration turned to anger can be political. Anger that comes from helplessness often turns inward as guilt and self-hatred. But it can also be turned around and directed against the social institutions and attitudes that have made the epidemic more horrible than it would have been without homophobia, class prejudice, and laissez-faire medicine. The political anger that's good for the sanity of the individual is also good for changing the body politic. Used in fiction, it can even produce powerful writing.

The first, most famous, and still most effective use of political anger in AIDS fiction is *The Normal Heart* by Larry Kramer. A dramatized documentary of Kramer's confrontations with friends, the media, the gay community, and the New York City mayor's office over AIDS, the play is one of those rare literary works that function as news while remaining art. When it opened in 1985, the play seemed like raw news, necessary yet artless. Rereading *The Normal Heart* five years later, I'm struck by how dramatically strong the play is, especially in its critical, honest treatment of the protagonist, Ned Weeks. Ned is not just a mouthpiece for Kramer, for the purposes of the play he *is* Kramer, complete with the flaw of angry righteousness that makes people resist both the real man and his fictional counterpart. Ned is a fully fleshed character, with room for us to reject him, so that *The Normal Heart* has a powerful subject that outlasts the play's original value as a call to arms.

A factor affecting my rereading of Kramer is that his anger was ahead of its time. Until recently, political anger in other AIDS fiction was limited to stray outbursts by isolated characters. Entering the 1990s, we suddenly have an enraged AIDS activist in Paul Monette's *Afterlife*, an AIDS activist group similar to ACT UP in Sarah Schulman's *People in Trouble*, and a roomful of angry PWAs in Joe Pintauro's play *Raft of the Medusa*. This eruption of anger in fiction is not due simply to the existence of groups like ACT UP. Fiction has developed alongside reality. The seven years needed for anger over the inept, often criminal response to AIDS by the government to coalesce into a political movement has its literary equivalent in the time needed for writers to trust themselves with anger and find appropriate methods for using it.

Pintauro's *Raft* uses the deceptively simple theatrical device of a support group for PWAs to divide its anger among twelve different characters. Less than a third of the group are gay white men; the others are women, people of color, bisexuals, addicts, and ex-cons. They are imagined as individuals as well as types, but their seizing of each other as the nearest available targets for anger and blame dramatizes the rifts of class and race exacerbated by AIDS. Yet, the disease that sets them against each other also bonds them, and their anger is also directed outward, at government negligence, public apathy, and, finally, the passive fascination of those intrigued by the drama of their pain, which means the audience and even the playwright. This is art that questions its right to address its subject, yet goes on to address it with harrowing power and sympathy.

The charge that art is not enough is at the center of Schulman's *People in Trouble*. This novel, too, deals with social inequality violently deepened by the epidemic, then shows the wrongs being fought through organized protest. Schulman sidesteps some of the pitfalls of agit-prop by telling her story through a love affair between two women, Kate, a painter whose husband smugly waits for her to grow bored with lesbianism, and Molly, a younger, politically committed woman who works with the homeless. Both women become involved with an AIDS activist group called Justice, Kate more for the intoxication of standing on the barricades than out of real belief or compassion. Kate uses her excitement in her painting, then breaks off with Molly and abandons activism for other art projects. Molly continues the work of protest without her. Weakening the novel's clear choice of political action is the fact that its activist scenes have less weight and complexity than the love affair. This might be due to Schulman's decision to treat social wrongs in the shorthand of satirical fantasy, or maybe fiction simply does the personal better than it does the public. One could even argue that the failure of the politics as fiction fits in with the rejection of art for action. The reader must go out into the world to complete this novel for him or herself.

These are some of the means and ends in writing fiction about AIDS that take us beyond the death of Little Nell. Most fiction mixes approaches. *Raft of the Medusa* closes with a fantasy dance among its antagonists; "The *Times* as It Knows Us" deftly uses comedy to nail self-serving behavior as well as catch the mixed feelings the narrator sustains under his frustration; the comic fantasy of *Angels in America* carries its own load of political anger. I should also mention the formalist approach, a concentration on literary technique and structure used by White, Barnett, and others to avoid melodrama, but carried to its furthest extreme by Susan Sontag in her story "The Way We Live Now," where a long illness is reported solely through the remarks of a circle of disembodied voices. I respect Sontag's story but distrust its cold brilliance. Unlike White and Barnett, there's little I can take from Sontag except admiration for her brilliance, and the fear that this is how the general population experiences the epidemic: snatches of gossip overheard in the distance.

There are many works I haven't mentioned, but, as the samples suggest, almost all AIDS fiction is about gay men. No, AIDS is not just a gay disease. In the United States, however, AIDS fiction is almost exclusively gay fiction. The exceptions are few and most of those are written from a gay and lesbian perspective that reaches out to other communities. Nobody wants to think too much about the epidemic. Gay men and their friends do so only because our lives and mental health depend on it, so we're the ones who write and read the books.

And we do read them, not in large quantities but always with care and deliberation. I meet gay men who refuse to read anything about AIDS, some out of cowardice, others with good cause—they work with the sick or are sick themselves. But sooner or later, even those who refuse will pick up a novel or see a play. Nobody reads everything, or should want to. I find myself reading AIDS fiction in bursts, two or three books at a time, or I burn out on the subject and become anxious and panicky, or, worse, numb. I take books reluctantly, like medicine, to enable myself to think about things I'd rather not think about yet know I must, if I want to stay sane and human.

One advantage to writing within a minority group is you get some idea of who your readers are and how they're using your books. My first novel, *Surprising Myself*, brought me sunny mail from young men just coming out or entering a relationship. The response to *Angel Clare* has been very different. There have been fewer letters, but they're more serious, well considered and experienced. I feel guilty for having written the book. I'm proud of it, too, yet writing *Angel Clare* purged nothing and I often wonder what good it might do readers. But one man wrote me, at the end of a frank letter about the loss of a friend, "Your book did not give me any answers . . . but it did give me the warm feeling I was not alone in these complicated times." Which might not sound like much, but it is. Twenty years ago, men and women combed libraries for novels that could tell them a simple truth they couldn't find elsewhere: You are not alone. Now we have access to a rich, complex literature that tells us we're not alone in grief, confusion, or anger.

Actually, I believe AIDS fiction does more than that. Through the remove of fiction one can confront hard emotions that, repressed or ignored, leave people emotionally dead or violently self-destructive. Fears examined while following the experience of strangers who exist only on the printed page lose some of their irrational power—reasonable fears are bad enough. The calm objectivity, judicious black comedy, and critical anger that function as defenses against pathos in the fiction become bulwarks against panic and hopelessness when translated to a reader's life.

Literature as therapy seems a small thing compared to ideals of timeless art or the need for political change, but this is a valid and necessary role for fiction, its first, most basic step. In the private office of story, a writer and reader try to loosen the clench of the times they live in. What begins in intimate confidences might end in art or politics or both. AIDS fiction is as personally connected to the world at hand as the writing of Lorraine Hansberry and James Baldwin was to the Civil

Rights movement, or *The Grapes of Wrath* was to the Great Depression, or the poem "Easter 1916" was to the Dublin uprising that confused Yeats with horror for its violence and admiration of the participants. "Too long a sacrifice," Yeats wrote there, "can make a stone of the heart." Which brings us back to Oscar Wilde on pathos and Little Nell: AIDS fiction is written and read in an effort to keep hearts from turning to stones.

1992

FAGGOTS REVISITED

—⁓—

T HE TITLE ALONE was a slap in the face. The word has lost some of its sting, but imagine an African-American novel titled *Niggers* or one by a woman called *Cunts*. The book itself hit many gay readers like a slap in 1978. The angry responses ranged from George Whitmore declaring in *The Body Politic* that copies should be burned, to the graffiti I saw in the john of my local gay bar: "If brevity is the soul of wit, *Faggots* is witless."

Few novels make such an impact that they get reviewed on bathroom walls. This was one of those highly public books that people could judge without reading, yet it was a bestseller, read by many and often enjoyed. And it was remembered, branding Kramer with a reputation for hating his sexuality, or at least for hating sex. His satire of high ghetto life clearly treated the new sexual freedom as foolish, shoddy, even soul-killing. Three years later, when Kramer's first AIDS piece ran in the *New York Native*, "A Personal Appeal," skeptics used the novel to dismiss his proposal that 120 cases of a "gay cancer" might be the start of a catastrophe. Playwright Robert Chesley wrote an open letter that accused him of having always believed "the wages of gay sin are death." As late as 1991, when the brutal fact of AIDS was undeniable, an academic critic argued, "Kramer could address AIDS with such speed and force because the disease served as an objective correlative for many of the ideas and attitudes he already had"—the unfortunate use of a term from literary criticism suggesting that Kramer would have "written" the epidemic if it hadn't already existed.

Novels rarely sustain such long, controversial lives. If they irritate, they usually disappear forever, or drop from view for a few generations, like *The Bostonians*, Henry James's satire of the sex wars, or are quickly tamed into "classics," as happened with Richard Wright's raw racial thriller, *Native Son*. Certainly no gay novel has elicited such prolonged, strong feelings from its audience. If the book provoked so much anger, why didn't it simply go away? What does it mean to us now, eighteen years later?

We should go back to the novel itself, before it became a myth. After all, it began as just another work of fiction.

Faggots is a 384-page comedy about a Memorial Day weekend in the early seventies among New York City's gay elite, an elastic aristocracy of libido, beauty, youth, and/or money. At the center is thirty-nine-year-old Fred Lemish, a screenwriter trying to set up a motion picture about this new gay world while he pursues the love of his life, Dinky Adams. Around them are hundreds of other gay characters, the densely populated book suspended between two mammoth parties, one the opening of a new club, the Toilet Bowl, the other the first party of the season on Fire Island. Along the way are orgies, a fire in a bathhouse, a public fistfuck in the Pines, and much casual tricking.

Kramer has claimed Evelyn Waugh was his model, and there is evidence of Waugh in the floor plan, not *Brideshead Revisited* or *The Loved One*, but the perpetual party of "Bright Young Things" in his 1930 novel, *Vile Bodies*. The book built on that foundation, however, has none of the restraint of Waugh's deadpan comedy, but belongs to the maximalist fiction of the sixties, those inventive three-ring circuses overloaded with people, plots, subplots, speeches, and wordplay, content overflowing form. The novel looks back to *V* and *Gravity's Rainbow* by Thomas Pynchon, the mega-narratives of John Barth, the word-drunk tapdance of *The Armies of the Night* by Norman Mailer. And it looks ahead to Tom Wolfe's 1987 novel, *The Bonfire of the Vanities*, the resemblance so strong that one can't help wondering if *Faggots* were a model for Wolfe's book. Both are comic jeremiads, cartoon extravaganzas where New York City is treated as a vast stageset. Wolfe includes a broader range of class and race, and is more obsessed with fashion and furniture than his gay counterpart. Yet the chief difference between the two works, a profound one, is Kramer's self-critical awareness, an acknowledgment of complicity that's completely absent in Wolfe's zoo of rip-off artists. Wolfe stands at a safe distance from his prejudged characters, while Kramer scatters naked, contradictory pieces of himself throughout his cast.

Faggots employs a busy mock-eighteenth-century narrative voice, a device rediscovered in the sixties as an alternative to the button-down conventions of cinematic realism. The prose is full of deliberately absurd names, odd capitalization, eccentric punctuation, bits of S. J. Perelman punning, and many jokes, both good and bad. Much of this sits heavily on the page for the first hundred pages while scene and characters are introduced. Kramer's talent is dramatic, not verbal, which is not to say that he's primarily a playwright, but that his art needs action, the bounce of opposing personas in collision to come to life. He needs the momentum of plot to keep his attitudes, caricatures and often heavy jokes airborne. It takes time for the carnival machinery of the novel to get underway.

This slow opening turned me against the book the first time I tried to read it. I have since learned that I am not the only person to put it down after twenty or thirty pages. And I disliked its sexual bluntness, the emphasis on the dirt rather than the poetry of sex. The epigraph from Waugh—". . . the ancients located the deeper emotions in the bowels"—is not there for nothing. I moved to New York the year that *Faggots* came out and the description of something called "felching" on page three wasn't what a young man from the provinces wanted to hear about. Not until several years later, when I'd had enough sexual experience to get over my squeamishness and see past the scatology to the sheer energy of the book, could I actually read it through.

The novel doesn't fully take off until the arrival of Timmy Purvis, a sixteen-year-old boy literally fresh off the bus from suburban Maryland. Timmy introduces joy to the novel, a selfish exuberance with none of the bad conscience of Fred and his friends. As Timmy and the others carom from party to party, dick to dick, the novel develops a velocity that carries through to the end. An elaborate logistics of parties, chance encounters and copulations has been worked out to create an erotic Rube Goldberg machine. Timmy meets his dream lover, Winnie the Winston man; the two fall into a feckless dance of lust and distraction, until Timmy falls into the hands of the sadistic, closeted media executive, Randy Dildough. Fred pursues Dinky, Dinky pursues new thrills. Fred brings Abe Bronstein, his producer and the novel's straight father figure, to the Toilet Bowl and out to Fire Island to see this brave new world. Meanwhile Bronstein's gay son, Boo Boo, plots his own kidnapping to get ransom money from his father. A multitude of other characters plan conquests, romance, financial gain, and just getting laid.

Soul-killing or not, casual sex among a huge all-male cast can't help but reduce characters to a faceless swarm. (The females are minor, although there's a surprisingly sweet subplot about a lesbian fling by Bronstein's ex-wife, Ephra.) The important figures read clearly, however, and this melding of identities is one of the novel's subjects. You have to go back to the gleeful absurdities of French eighteenth-century pornography to find a similar mix of slapstick, philosophy, and fucking. The sex itself is rarely sinister. For all these men's macho role-playing, only the self-hating Randy Dildough is deliberately vicious, and even his cruelty comes out of a desperate romantic need. Despite their self-indulgence, these men usually *mean* well. The flood of diminutive nicknames—Dinky, Timmy, Boo Boo—conjures up a world of good little boys playing at toughness, escaping inhibitions with fantasies, costumes, and drugs. (The novel's delirium is fueled by a remarkable intake of chemicals, more striking now than when it was first published.)

We cannot forget that *Faggots* is a comedy, which should allow for exaggeration and some unfairness. But comedy is slippery, subjective; it needs surprise to get away with the murder it seeks to commit. Kramer often succeeds, but his humor is uneven, with the hit-or-miss quality of rude jokes by a teenager suddenly free to say anything. The title, for example, is intended, in part, as a nose-thumbing joke, only who exactly is meant to be laughing? The comic names can be obvious, stale or just plain silly. As with most broad comedy, there is much stereotyping. Italians, African-Americans, and WASPs all get caricatured—square-jawed blonds are mocked for their blandness, although they remain the standard of beauty—but the heaviest artillery, sometimes clever, sometimes crude, is reserved for Jews, like Kramer himself. He's an equal-opportunity mocker. (A detail that still disturbs me, however, is his "Ubangi-lipped" urinal.)

This adolescent comedy was of its time, when the joke was on propriety and just voicing the outrageous seemed funny to some people. The failed jokes here are no worse than those in other Seventies comedies, such as *The Great American Novel* by Philip Roth or *Breakfast of Champions* by Kurt Vonnegut, two veteran authors. *Faggots* was a first novel. Kramer was forty-four when it appeared, but the book reads like the first work of a younger man, excessive and vulgar, yet also lively, boisterous, and passionate. It commits almost every literary sin imaginable, except the fatal ones of being either dull or trivial.

The mass of incidents is held together by the chain reaction of sexual encounters, and a single issue, introduced early in the thoughts of Jack Humpstone, a teacher who's part-owner of a gay club: "Yes, sex and love were different items when he wanted them in one, and yes, having so much sex made having love impossible, and yes, sadism was only a way to keep people away from us and masochism only a way to clutch them close, and yes, we are sadists with some guys and masochists with other guys and sometimes both with both, and yes, we're all out of the closet but we're still in the ghetto and all I see are guys hurting each other and themselves." Jack is feeling burned by the end of his six-year relationship with the elusive, thrill-obsessed Dinky. His ideas are the very ones that Fred will come to believe once Dinky finishes with him. Jack functions as an alter ego to Fred, who's already an alter ego of the author.

There are two novels here, or rather, two contrasting tones. The first, focused on Fred and supported by Jack, is full of dissatisfaction with the sexual feeding frenzy. The other, centered around the adventures of Timmy Purvis, is a sharp, irresponsible comedy that captures the sheer joy of humping any stranger who responds to your smile. Even Fred drops into this erotic pinball game now and then, and it can be very sexy. I've talked to men who found *Faggots* quite hot when it came out and used it for one-handed reading, despite its message.

There is no denying where Kramer himself stands in his satire, but he complicates his argument. In addition to the sexiness of the book is the comedy of Fred's hypocrisy and, by extension, the author's. Kramer recognizes the irony of writing a fat, sex-driven novel that denounces sex. He puts that comic hypocrisy in the foreground during the exchange between Fred and Dinky on the eve of the party at Fire Island, a dialogue that's the didactic center of the book, and frequently quoted by Kramer's critics. It's here that Fred tells Dinky gay men need to discover committed love, "Before you fuck yourself to death"—a line later read as a prophecy of AIDS. Fred wants Dinky to be his lover. Dinky wants only to be friends and accuses Fred of aping heterosexual marriage. While they talk, Dinky suits up for the night's orgy, slipping on cock rings, leather vest, and boots. Fred can't take his eyes off Dinky while he delivers his big speech:

> "I'm tired of being a New York City–Fire Island faggot, I'm tired of using my body as a faceless thing to lure another faceless thing, I want to love a Person!, I want to go out and live in that world with that Person, a Person who loves me, we shouldn't *have* to be faithful, we should *want* to be faithful, love grows, sex gets better, if you don't drain all your fucking energy off somewhere else, no, I don't want you to neutralize us into a friendship!, for all of the above! . . . stop running away from me and yourself and answer me . . . and. . . uhn . . . where did you say you bought the boots?"

Because, despite his high-sounding words, Fred is excited by the sight of Dinky in leather. The appeal of that fantasy makes him wonder if his ideal of marriage is fantasy, too. He fights his doubt and plunges on, but the comedy at his expense rattles his soapbox, makes him more human.

Kramer gives Dinky good arguments against romantic monogamy, including the fact that neither of them know any happy straight marriages. This is reinforced by our glimpses of Fred's parents, a cartoon version of the family that Kramer later explored with real pain and sympathy in *The Destiny of Me*. Even Abe Bronstein, the good, straight father, has had more marriages than he can keep count of.

But the strongest argument against Fred's belief that love is the answer comes not in words but action, in the most powerful scene in the book, the public fistfuck in the woods on Fire Island. Fred, still angrily in love with Dinky, watches with a hundred other men while the object of his affection is hoisted in a swing and fisted by Dinky's other resentful lover, Jack Humpstone. The play-acted violence comes dangerously close to what both men actually feel: Jack would like to kill Dinky; Fred would like to see him die. Jack thinks, "Yes, I could punch a hole in your stomach just like you punched a hole in the last six years of my life." The reader holds his breath while Jack strains to keep his anger in check. Kramer prolongs the scene in a suspenseful knot of unrequited love and deadly anger. What kind of love is it, though, where you want to destroy the beloved if you cannot possess him? Such love is just as soul-killing as the obliteration of self in pleasure.

This is a novel written by a writer divided against himself, arguing with himself, a split that continues to give the book surprising power. In an anti-sex climate, it would still be controversial. For all its faults, *Faggots* remains alive as few books do so many years after publication.

Why were the gay press and many gay readers so righteously indignant when *Faggots* first appeared?

Political timing was a factor. This was one year after the Anita Bryant campaign in Miami, when the religious right used fake statistics and accounts of bizarre sex acts to revoke Dade County's gay rights code. A similar battle was underway in 1978 over the Briggs Amendment in California, which would have barred gay people from teaching in public schools. At the very moment when activists were arguing that gay men were no kinkier than anyone else, a major publisher put out a commercial novel that opens with two men inviting the protagonist to piss on them. Reviews in the mainstream—the *Los Angeles Times*, for example—harped on this bad public image as much as the gay press did. (To my knowledge, the religious right has never quoted the novel in its campaigns, although Midge Decter cited it in her smug 1980 *Commentary* essay, "The Boys on the Beach.")

Deeper than current events and fears about image, however, was the fact that *Faggots* hit a nerve with gay readers. If they were as comfortable with the sexual free-for-all as they claimed, they could have dismissed the book with, "Oh, Larry, relax." But their feelings were every bit as split as Kramer's. A friend hated the book simply because it told people like his parents what he did in the backrooms and the docks every weekend; he was ashamed to have his secret life publicized. Such embarrassment masked larger frustrations with this world of available skin.

At the time, the new pride of the seventies seemed to be built on sexual freedom. To cast doubt on sex was to doubt the value of liberation. Yet we forget that gay promiscuity, anonymous sex, sex-for-the-sake-of-sex (none of the phrases feel right) was not a post-Stonewall invention. Read any account of the period between 1945 and 1969, the journals of Christopher Isherwood or Donald Vining, for example, or biographies of Frank O'Hara and Tennessee Williams. When sex was one of the few available social acts for gay men, there was plenty of sex. Gay liberation, along with the relaxing of liquor laws, the growth of bars and backrooms, and the pleasure revolution that affected everyone in the sixties, only turned up the volume, transforming an established custom into a frenzied institution with its own ideology.

This ideology is difficult to discuss when it was more often implied than articulated. Sex is intensely subjective anyway, full of built-in guilt and anxiety. No matter what you do or don't do, it often feels wrong. During my first years in New York, I felt that I'd failed as a gay man if I didn't have X number of partners over Y span of time—I use algebra because the numbers too were purely subjective. Monogamy was considered a blind aping of heterosexuals, despite the fact that the sexual revolution made fidelity less mandatory for them as well. Of course there were monogamous gay couples, and many men visited the fleshpots only in concentrated bursts. Sexual adventure can be exhausting, especially if you have a full time job. Then came AIDS, which made monogamy acceptable, even respectable.

Nineteen seventy-eight was the miracle year of gay male fiction. *Faggots* appeared within months of *Dancer from the Dance* by Andrew Holleran and *Nocturnes for the King of Naples* by Edmund White, along with Armistead Maupin's sunnier, saner *Tales of the City*. Kramer was singled out as the glum, self-loathing brother. Nevertheless, Holleran and White carry their own load of regret and unease. Holleran's discontent is expressed in romantic elegy over the impossibility of love; White internalizes his dissatisfaction in a wounded narrator who sleepwalks through an imaginary world that bears only traces of the seventies. (White's self-chastisement continued in his next novels with less metaphorical plumage; it's especially strong in *The Beautiful Room Is Empty*. His essays reprinted in *The Burning Library* present sport sex as all fun and games, but his fiction paints a darker picture.) Kramer was not the only one with doubts about this artificial paradise, but he was more blunt than White or Holleran in his meanings, more raw and artless. Minorities are quick to attack the first pictures of their lives, demanding that they be both positive and universal. Gay critics may have pounced on the other novels if *Faggots* hadn't been there to serve as a lightning rod.

Eighteen years later, the secret war between domestic love and Dionysian sex has still not worked itself out. Put on hold during the epidemic, the debate became frozen, exaggerated. The ideology of sex was tamed in campaigns for safe sex, translated into a need for pornography, underwear parties, and j.o. clubs. Recently, it's been readdressed as a fear that younger men are having unsafe sex again. The debate is complicated by the fact that different generations are involved. Men in their twenties and thirties do most of the fucking; older men do most of the pontificating, projecting their ideological fantasies on the young. Gabriel Rotello righteously denounces the wild life he once enjoyed, while Leo Bersani and Frank Browning rhapsodize over it as the one true homosexuality.

Is promiscuity soul-killing? Or is it the keystone of gay identity? Monogamy or soullessness? Sexual freedom or surrender to mainstream hypocrisy? Such an extreme either/or, which is at the center of the *Faggots* controversy, resembles the all-or-nothing approach that alcoholics must use with booze. There has to be a looser, more flexible way to think about sex. In the seventies we took a perfectly human desire to fuck around occasionally and recast it as one of George Orwell's "smelly little orthodoxies." It was the most efficient defense against very mixed feelings that included guilt and broken hearts. But the celebration of monogamous love as the chief aim of adult life is also a defense mechanism. Love is work, life in a couple isn't always sane or virtuous, and the world is full of lighter, brighter opportunities. I should say here that I've been with the same man now for sixteen years. I am continually surprised at the life we've made together, how we both feel better grounded in this thicker, heavier, shared existence. Yet I don't believe for a minute that our bond makes us better, or worse, than our single friends.

What is the answer? I don't know, unless it's simply that there is no answer. Any public declaration about something as private as sex will be wrong. Dig deep enough into *Faggots* and you find a similar message. Trust the tale, not the teller. Yes, the novel attacks the ideology of sex, but it also casts doubts on the ideology of love.

A romantic moralist, Kramer has an undeniable squint, but one that enabled him to see past false pride and nervous guilt to question customs still at the center of gay life. *Faggots* remains important as a tool for arguing about the role of sex in our cultural identity. It has become part of our common language. We improve our vocabulary by seeing the difficult, ambiguous, living book that's actually there, rather than the simplistic Paradise Lost/Paradise Scorned of its reputation.

The novel has also become important as a chapter in the ongoing work-in-progress that is Larry Kramer. *Faggots* would not be nearly as meaningful, or as interesting, if its author disappeared after writing it. We use this man in a variety of ways, as a spokesperson, scapegoat, guilty conscience, hero, and villain. We use him to think about our lives.

A public figure as well as an autobiographical writer, Kramer has shared more private life with the world than is safe for anyone. Two years ago, word went out in gay literary circles that he had found a boyfriend. He was setting up house with a man whom he had known years before: the very man, in fact, who was the model for Dinky Adams. Dinky didn't fuck himself to death after all. What next? How important is sex and fidelity to these two men now that they're older? What does requited love mean to someone who believed in it so fervently and wanted it for so long? Will the day-to-day compromises of domestic life make him looser and more flexible? Was love the answer?

Postscript (Group Reading, Different Light Bookstore, January 28, 1998)

I WILL NOT be reading from my essay *"Faggots* Revisited." I wrote it a year and a half ago. I still stand by most of what I say there. But what a difference a year and a half makes.

It's a truth universally acknowledged that Larry Kramer has a remarkable gift for pissing people off. Once our anger passes, we joke about it, which might be a mistake but is probably the sanest way to deal with our mixed feelings about this prickly, energetic, large-souled man. Well, the publication of this book catches me in mid-piss. Reading the other contributors, I find I am hardly the first angry admirer, and have less cause for fury than many. But I wonder if the book might not be better titled, *We Must Love Larry Kramer, Even When He Bites Our Heads Off.*

My anger began last spring with his essay in the *Advocate,* "Sex and Sensibility." As you all know, that was mostly an attack on the new Ed White novel, three months before it was published, for being one long fuckfest. And yes, White's book has a lot of sex, although not nearly as much as *Faggots,* and the very things that Kramer complained were missing—family, homophobia, career—are all there. I have my own problems with the book, but it's a serious, complex novel. It's hard to believe that Kramer read anything except the dirty parts. He then went on to trash all gay male fiction for being nothing but dirty parts. He trashed a recent anthology of coming-out stories, without naming it, for being all first lays. Well, I've read that anthology—I'm in it, in fact—and one of many surprising things about the collection—*Boys Like Us,* edited by

Patrick Merla, who also has a piece in tonight's book—is that less than half the stories turn on first times, and those that do all treat the encounters as part of larger dramas. I can't believe Kramer read that book either.

I find it hard to believe he's read much gay fiction at all. There are plenty of writers who address other things besides sex—Allan Gurganus, Michael Nava, Dale Peck, Michael Cunningham, Randall Kenan, myself—it gets silly when you start naming them—or who write through sex to the rest of life, because sex is rarely a simple, isolated event. In fact, it's hard to write truthfully about gay life, or straight life for that matter, without getting into sex.

My anger was not because I felt personally attacked. No, I got sniped at only recently, quite mildly, in the interview here, where Kramer slaps me, Mark Merlis, and Dale Peck on our wrists for not writing fatter, more ambitious novels, presumably like the one he's been working on all these years. Mark, incidentally, also has a piece in this book. No, what infuriated me about the *Advocate* essay was that I'd just written a long piece that tried to give a close, fair reading to *Faggots*, only to find its author was incapable of doing the same for any of us. Simple Episcopal boy from Virginia that I am, a firm believer in do-unto-others, what-goes-around-comes-around, I felt like a total putz.

I wrote "*Faggots* Revisited" for two reasons. First, I wanted to describe what's actually in Kramer's novel, not the one-note anti-sex rant of reputation, but the thing itself, its energetic storytelling and dramatic, many-sided arguments and attitudes that have kept the book alive all these years.

Second, I wanted to use the novel and the attacks on it to look at our dangerously limited way of thinking about the role of sex in gay life. The debate over *Faggots* in 1978 fell into an extreme either/or: sex—meaning casual sex, non-mongamous sex, sex-for-fun, sex-to-meet-people, whatever we call it—was the keystone and touchstone of gay identity; or it was the shame of gay life, an awful, corrosive, selfish thing that made love and community impossible. I argue that we need to find a middle way between these extremes, an approach that integrates sex into the rest of life. I even claim, naively perhaps, that for all its sermons and tirades, one can read a similar call in *Faggots*. After all, here was a sex-drenched, sex-powered, sex-obsessed book denouncing sex. Clearly Kramer had his own mixed feelings.

This old debate over sex never entirely disappeared. AIDS, however, changed its terms. In a strange way, it put the debate on hold. People didn't denounce sex as evil in itself anymore, but as a health emergency. The call for sexual freedom was tamed into safe-sex campaigns. The righteous, bitter moralizing went out of the argument, until recently.

The war started up again shortly after new AIDS treatments led some foolish people to declare that the epidemic was over. First we had articles by Rotello and Signorile, then whole books by them, attacking the excessive amount of sex in gay life. Then there was Kramer's essay in the *Advocate*, attacking the excessive sex in gay fiction. Then, in response to these attacks, plus the closing down of clubs and bars in New York and reported rise in police harassment, a handful of activists, writers, and teachers formed a group called Sex Panic to argue with this Puritanism.

So we're back in the old either/or debate from the time of *Faggots*. Only it doesn't play the way I thought it would.

There has been a lot of misrepresentation by both sides. You might say Sex Panic started it by criticizing Rotello, Signorile, and Kramer, calling them the nastiest name gay men in New York can call one another: neoconservatives. Yet that was not their whole program, despite what the criticized critics claim—and Hell hath no fury like a criticized critic. You'd never know, reading Rotello, Signorile, and Kramer, that Sex Panic believes strongly in HIV prevention. I don't agree with everything they say. It's a small ad hoc group of different voices—one cannot overemphasize how ad hoc it is—including a couple who spout the old promiscuity-is-the-heart-of-gay-identity nonsense—inevitably quoted in the mainstream. But the majority, some with backgrounds in health and counseling, are careful, responsible and sane.

I am forty-five years old. I am part of a couple. Bars and clubs play no role in my life. This is not my fight. But I have to say that Sex Panic comes closer to the middle way I want than their opponents do. In fact, I'd go so far as to claim that they're the conservatives here (in the good meaning of the word), wanting to preserve, improve, and deepen existing safe sex programs, recognizing that there's more danger in making sex a dirty, guilty secret again than in treating it as a natural part of gay men's lives.

Kramer himself delivered the ugliest blow in this war of words last month on the editorial page of the *Times*, where he

presented Sex Panic as the wild-eyed advocates of unsafe prac-
tices, mandatory promiscuity, and—one of his obsessions—
fucking in public toilets. What made this piece especially nasty
is that it's all many people, gay as well as straight, now know
of the group. Kramer likes to call himself a voice crying in the
wilderness, but, as a friend puts it, his wilderness is the op-ed
page of the *New York Times*.

Some hope such rhetoric will force a dialogue, but Kramer
himself does not appear to want that. There are reports that
he campaigned to have the editor of a prominent gay magazine replaced because she was a woman and didn't understand men's issues. Her lack of understanding had become
evident when she allowed *both* sides of the debate to be heard.
The word on the street is that Sarah Petitt was fired for more
trivial reasons, but it's an ugly business when merely letting
your opponent speak is treated as an irresponsible crime.

I once believed that Larry Kramer was an intelligent,
moral man who had to lose it now and then in order to say
what needed to be said. I hope to believe that again in time.
Beneath the distortion and hyperbole of his earlier attacks—
on GMHC, on ACT UP, on all of us—there was always a clear
moral purpose that one agreed with, even if one disliked the
package. This year, however, I can find no valid goal in his
words or deeds, only an aimless irritability. He keeps remind-
ing me of Cyril Connolly's description of a mad elephant in
an Indian village, who, with equal fervor, charges first a man,
then a truck, then swings around to chase a chicken.

It's frustrating, and sad, when someone you admire, for
all his difficulties, becomes so difficult that you can no longer

give him the benefit of the doubt. Whatever the cause for his current state of mind, I hope he snaps out of it soon. But then, Larry was always easier to admire during those periods when he kept his mouth shut.

1996–1998

MAPPING THE TERRITORY:
GAY MEN'S WRITING

—⁓—

1

F OR THE LONGEST time, gay men and
women seemed to be a community of the
book, at least on weeknights when we weren't
a community of the bar. With all other public
forums closed to us, we searched the libraries for titles that would tell us a simple truth:
You are not alone. The books were never so
important as when they were so few—even
though, more often than not, the truth came
disguised as sad morality tales or shelved
under "Psychology, Abnormal."

The great change began roughly twenty years ago, in both the books and the people who read them. The flowering of gay and lesbian writing has been astounding, an literary explosion that is positively uncanny in an age that many critics consider postliterate. It was part of a larger explosion, of course. We are not only a people of many books now, but of parades, political campaigns, PAC funds, and TV commercials. The literature has become as wide and diverse as the communities that make and use it. A remarkable variety is suggested by this book of Robert Giard's photographs, a dense forest of American faces.

One is tempted just to stroll through the forest and point out favorite trees. Each picture represents a unique combination of experience, talent, and achievement. All that these people have in common is that they write, and they're gay, and some are extraordinary. But one can't help wanting to sketch a map of the forest in an attempt to understand where we are.

Joan Nestle and I have divided the challenge of offering an overview by gender. But we are not on separate planets. When I first began to read as a gay man, wanting to see what my life might be like, I found pieces of myself in Jane Rule and Adrienne Rich that were missing in John Rechy and Allen Ginsberg. I know several women who get the rest of their story from reading men. We complete each other's work, and gender is no more a barrier here than it is—or should be—in the world at large.

2

WHAT IS GAY literature?

Most authors dislike the very notion, although few still bristle at being called "gay writers." The smart ones respond with jokes. "A gay play is any play that wants to sleep with another play of its gender," quipped playwright Robert Patrick. Such wisecracks come out of anxiety. Writers want to work their private visions for the largest audience possible. The idea of "literature" is narrow enough without an adjective attached. And writing within any minority group has a noisome political burden. We're expected to provide witnesses for the defense and even the prosecution, when what we really want to do is offer new words that everyone will remember long after a particular trial is over.

Nevertheless, the best working definition of gay literature might be that it's the fiction, poetry, drama, history, and essays written by, about, and for gay men.

All three prepositions are slippery. Does John Cheever qualify as a gay author? Just how gay are James Purdy's characters? The last, however, *for*, is the trickiest, and perhaps the most important. It posits an audience, part community, part market, something to support a writer's gamble that readers exist who will understand him, who can be moved, disturbed, soothed, or confronted in the most meaningful ways. Other readers are welcomed and the relationship is not exclusive. But as a writer myself, I feel that my first audience are those who have been in places of heart and mind that I know firsthand. I strive to write about equals for my equals, without condescension, apology, or stale preconception. It makes me more honest.

3

WE NEED A history of readers as well as authors.

The early poems and novels often look like those proverbial trees that crash silently when nobody is around to hear. Yet there was an audience even before the writers dared to admit it. John Addington Symonds thought he'd discovered a fellow soul in *Leaves of Grass*, although when he wrote to Walt Whitman, repeatedly, the Good Gray Poet lied, refusing to sacrifice his hard-earned fame to be the figurehead of a secret society. Men who were "like that" recommended *The Picture of Dorian Gray* to each other—and even some critics understood what Oscar Wilde's novel was really about, one reviewer claiming the tale would interest only outlawed lords and depraved telegraph boys.

It was an age of coded works, some more innocent than others. Herman Melville may have been unaware of how much he was revealing, but Henry James understood the stakes. Even Proust, who produced our first full picture of a gay communal underworld, pretended not to be writing about himself but creating an allegory of the universal fall, with inversion standing in for original sin. One could chronicle the literary use and abuse of homosexuality, from Balzac to Genet to Mishima, as not just a piece of life but an all-purpose metaphor for criminal ideas.

Proust, however, marks another important turning point: the

triumph of the autobiographical. In the chaos of the twentieth century, personal experience was seized as a rare patch of solid ground. Autobiography no longer hid in the machinery of three-decker novels or the formal conventions of poetry but became a subject in itself. Women wrote about their experience as women; the writers of the Harlem Renaissance, about black life. Even straight white men—and it's odd that more isn't made of this—no longer pretended to write about everyone but focused exclusively on their experience as straight white men. More and more often, when a male author loved men, it blatantly entered his work. Somerset Maugham managed to keep it out, but not André Gide or E. M. Forster—although he stashed those stories in a drawer—or the respectably married Thomas Mann.

There was a slow but steady accumulation of titles over the following decades. In the United States alone, we had *A Better Angel* (1933) by Foreman Brown, under the pseudonym of Richard Meeker, *The Young and the Evil* (1933) by Parker Tyler and Charles Henri Ford, *The Gallery* (1947) by John Horne Burns, *The City and the Pillar* (1949) by Gore Vidal, *Quatrefoil* (1950) by James Barr, *Giovanni's Room* (1956) by James Baldwin, *Howl and Other Poems* (1956) by Allen Ginsberg, *A Single Man* (1964) by Christopher Isherwood, *Totempole* (1965) by Sanford Friedman, *City of Night* (1966) by John Rechy, *The Boys in the Band* (1968) by Mart Crowley, *Selected Poems of Frank O'Hara* (1973), and *The Story of Harold* (1974) by George Selden, under the pseudonym of Terry Andrews. To the world outside, these works were often sensational nightmares or exotic case studies, but to those in the life they were partial yet badly needed mirrors of reality.

The great change only began with the 1969 Stonewall riots. Literature is rarely in sync with current events. The ground had to be prepared. The first half of the seventies saw the rise of gay newspapers, the growth of gay and lesbian bookstores, the birth of gay literary magazines and presses. Michael Denneny, one of the founders of *Christopher Street* magazine in 1976 with Charles Ortleb and Patrick Merla, has said that they expected to be inundated with a backlog of unpublished work. No, it was not until there was an outlet for such writing that most of it was written. The first successful gay male novel of the new era was *The Front Runner* (1973), whose author was a woman.

As is often noted, 1978 was the miracle year of gay letters, with the publication of *Dancer from the Dance* by Andrew Holleran, *Faggots* by Larry Kramer, and *Nocturnes for the King of Naples* by Edmund White, as well as *Tales of the City* by Armistead Maupin, *Splendora* by Edward Swift, and *The Family* by David Plante. The map suddenly changed; it was as if a whole new country had appeared. The predecessors went from being random curiosities to ancestors, forefathers.

This new country grew slowly at first. There was an attempt to create gay fiction by pouring homosexuality into old commercial molds. None of this genre writing took except for mysteries, a form already being explored by Joseph Hansen since *Skinflick* in 1970. An important twist to the story is that commercial gay fiction, gay trash if you will, did not succeed. Gay writing in all genres has had to have some seriousness and craft if it were to find readers. When gay men want trash, they buy the same potboilers as everyone else. Even our pornography tends to be better written than its heterosexual counterpart. Editors flopped around in a hunt for the next Andrew Holleran, assuming gay fiction must be about life in ghetto fast lanes. That assumption was loosened by the success of *The Family of Max Desir* by Robert Ferro in 1983, then broken for good with *Family Dancing* by David Leavitt in 1986. Publishing discovered the gay midlist novel. The books would not be bestsellers, but there was a small yet solid market for good, intelligent writing. Every house suddenly seemed to want a homosexual man or two in its catalog.

AIDS added further urgency to the work. Writers needed to write and, more important, readers needed to read about this new slow-motion cataclysm, desperate to name their fear, grief, and hope. Looking through these portraits, one cannot help being struck again by how many careers were cut short by the epidemic: George Whitmore, Charles Ludlam, Allen Barnett, Richard Hall, Roy Gonsalves, Alan Bowne, Melvin Dixon, John Preston, Manuel Ramos Otero, Stan Leventhal, Paul Monette, Essex Hemphill, and too, too many others. We cannot even guess at the careers silenced before they could begin.

Nevertheless, the literature continues to grow. It expands in new directions as more voices join in, gay men outside or straddling the ghetto, authors who bring with them other strong identities—racial, ethnic, religious—even sexualities that aren't strictly gay. When our commentators get sociological, they expect a hierarchical unity of gay life. The reality requires something closer to William James's treatment of religion, a *Varieties of Homosexual Experience*, which our poetry and prose have begun to provide.

4

WHEN WE DISCUSS authors, the natural tendency is to order them by generation: before Stonewall, after Stonewall, AIDS and beyond. Each group seems to work with and against what was produced by the preceding flight.

There's truth to that but it's not the full story. We talk about generations as if they come at ten- or even five-year intervals, ignoring the fact that it takes years to write a book, and most writers find voices and turfs long before they're published. Authors often don't know who their siblings are until after the fact. If the flurry of novels about gay men and their families in the eighties seemed like a reaction against the family-less novels of the seventies, it wasn't just the writers responding but the editors and reading public.

More important to a writer is the tradition he or she chooses to work in, the different sets of examples, styles, and strategies that run like currents through every genre. These streams are not timeless but do have surprising longevity. In mapping the territory, tradition can be used as the longitude to the latitude of generation.

Let me use literary fiction as an example. It's the area which I have thought about the most in an attempt to understand who I might be. Here's my list of contemporary traditions, illustrated with a sample of elders and peers:

a. The Avant Garde. Experiments and moods, prose that ranges from the shapely to the raw, with just a breath of story, often erotic, to keep the pieces aloft.

William Burroughs. Robert Gluck. Dennis Cooper. Sam D'Allesandro. (It says something about the strength of tradition that what we call the avant garde has retained much the same identity for at least fifty years.)

b. The Gothic. Fiction as expressionist fever dream, a dark unreality with its own nightmare truths. James Purdy. Truman Capote. Paul Bowles. Alfred Chester.

c. High Art. Fiction as beautiful, autonomous object, perfect sentences and cool control taking precedent— although emotion often slips in. Edmund White, Andrew Holleran. Robert Ferro. Christopher Coe. Matthew Stadler. Fenton Johnson.

d. Emotional realism. Good prose is still important but the emphasis is on character and feeling. Christopher Isherwood. James Baldwin. Jonathan Strong. David Leavitt. Allen Barnett. Melvin Dixon. Jaime Manrique. Lev Raphael. Michael Cunningham. Paul Reidinger. Philip Gambone. Paul Russell. Norman Wong. Paul Gervais. Mark Merlis. Scott Heim.

e. Comic realism. Story is more important, with a friendly looseness to the prose. Serious topics are touched on but the overall tone is good-humored. Armistead Maupin. Edward Swift. Stephen McCauley. David Feinberg. John Weir. Larry Duplechan.

f. Fabulism. An overload of story, character and invention, three-ring circuses where conventional structure and realism are ignored, although the emotion is often very real. Larry Kramer. Allan Gurganus. Tom Spanbauer. Randall Kenan. Peter Gadol.

Established traditions also play through poetry (the deceptive formality of Henri Cole or Timothy Liu, say, as opposed to the prosy conversation of Frank O'Hara and Walta Borowski or the fiery chants of Essex Hemphill and Assotto Saint) and playwriting (the subversive sitcom of Harvey Fierstein, the raw yet neatly sliced life of Joe Pintauro, the wild monologues of Luis Alfaro).

As with any game of categories, my breakdown of fiction can't help being debatable and even comic. There are writers like Dale Peck who merge traditions (gothic, high art, and fabulism) and others who change over time (Edmund White has shifted toward emotional realism). As for myself, I want to be an emotional realist but suspect I'm a comic realist and wonder if I might not be happier trying my hand at fabulism. Then there are writers in other genres whose work overlaps literary fiction. Michael Nava writes mysteries that are full of emotional realism. Lars Eighner's erotic tales touch on high art. Samuel R. Delany's science fantasy dances in and out all over the map.

Nevertheless, two truths emerge from this provisional list: First, at any given time, one tradition seems to hold sway. The gothic dominated before Stonewall, high art in the seventies and early eighties (political identity smuggled into literature in a gorgeous Trojan horse) and, this year at least, emotional realism. But the other important point the list makes is that no tradition ever quite disappears. There's always somebody out there practicing each one. Isherwood wrote plain-speak realism long before Stonewall. A writer in his twenties, Joey Manley, has returned to the gothic to play variations on Purdy and Capote.

Criticism tends to privilege one tradition over another, which is what makes this categorizing potentially pernicious.

Just as there's constant debate over whose homosexuality is more authentic, there is endless argument over what qualifies as true gay literature. Is Dennis Cooper, whose work crosses over to straight fans of the experimental, more gay than David Feinberg? Is Allan Gurganus, because his fiction contains such a broad range of sexualities, detrimentally less gay than Felice Picano? What constitutes the true subject of gay fiction? Coming out? Sexual adventure? Unrequited love? AIDS? All of the above?

These are cheater questions, shortcuts for judging books without having to read them. The truth is that good work can be done in any tradition, and bad work, too. And just when you're about to declare a branch dead, a writer comes along who breathes new life into it.

We also need to acknowledge that none of these traditions is strictly gay. There are pansexual kinships and influences. Edmund White is frequently compared to Vladimir Nabokov, for good reason. I hear the lessons of both Faulkner and García Márquez in Randall Kenan's books. So it goes outside fiction, too. Tony Kushner's polyphonic epics draw upon Shaw, Brecht, and, of course, Shakespeare. James Merrill's work is permeated with the enameled wit of Pope and Eliot. Mark Doty somehow marries Merrill with O'Hara, but I also catch Galway Kinnell's love of physical anarchy in his poems. There are echoes of Rilke in Bernard Cooper's essays, and of C. Vann Woodward and other literate historians in Martin Duberman's history.

More is happening here than new wine in old bottles. The bottles can be remarkably elastic. The strongest wine sometimes alters the shapes from within, so that certain traditions will never be the same.

5

THERE WAS ONCE something called the literary mainstream. Its recent demise is often mourned as a Balkanization of culture, as if books were now at war. I see the change as a badly needed case of decentralization. As recently as the seventies, any novel written by a woman about women was considered "women's fiction," parochial, or, worse, feminist. Forty years ago, African-American writing was treated as a side room defined solely by Richard Wright and Ralph Ellison, which was easy to do when so few other black authors were published. But in a world of books as diverse as the real world of men and women, boundaries begin to blur. We must recognize that, instead of a mainstream, there are many currents, a hundred tributaries that don't remain separate from each other or always flow in the same direction.

I believe that literary truth must be personal and local before it can have value for a wider audience. Working within a specific community anchors literature, gives it relevance and human scale. The best art often seems to come out of smaller city-states of culture: from Elizabethan London to the Italian and Japanese cinemas of the fifties and sixties to New York City's own Theater of the Ridiculous. Not coterie art, not in-crowd art, but art that looks hard through the particular to the general. As the century comes to a close, the writing of gay men, like that of women—both lesbian and straight—and racial minorities, brings a powerful electrical charge of personal experience and communal need to American culture.

Gay literature is a small yet miraculously vital country, a hothouse republic of letters, a country within a country, and not as foreign as it looks. If readers can find value in writers as strange and alien as Shakespeare, Marlowe, and Donne without being seventeenth-century Englishmen themselves, they certainly don't need to be gay to get emotion and insight from a poem by Thom Gunn or a story by Peter Cameron or a play by Victor Bumbalo.

As gay writers have learned from others, certainly non-gay readers can learn from us. We cultivate our own corners of the forest but are free to visit each other. We owe it to ourselves to visit. Difference, combined with curiosity, respect and empathy, can produce a living multidimensionality, like a landscape seen with a hundred different pairs of eyes.

1997

GEORGE AND AL

—⁓—

T HE FIRST IMAGE is a bedroom. Double mattress and box springs sit on the floor, under the window whose white security bars suggest a room in a mental hospital. It's the same bed Draper and I still share. Odd how much has and hasn't changed in eight years.

Credits, white on black: *George and Al.*

The bedroom again, another angle. A portable movie screen hangs on the wall over the bed, like an empty thought balloon in a comic strip.

Credits: *A Film by—*

Almost since the night we met, Draper and I talked about making movies. He was an art director and I worked in a bookstore, but we both loved films with a passion that could be requited only by making one. In our first years together, it was a bedtime story we told each other, concocting plots and scenes and characters while we lay under the blankets.

George and Al was our first film. It's thirty minutes long, shot in Super 8 and transferred to video. I wrote it, Draper directed it, and most of our friends became involved in one way or another. People often say that filmmaking is like being in a family, an intense yet temporary family that dissolves as soon as the project is completed. Because we worked with friends, this particular family preceded and survived its making.

It's a movie about making movies. Draper plays George, a gay man with a camera who thinks he can control his life if he gets it on film. We had a Super 8 sound camera. Draper loved the grainy texture and painterly colors, and I suggested we make the homemade roughness part of the story. A fictional documentary, the film consists entirely of footage shot with George's camera.

It begins with our empty bedroom, then morning-after glimpses of different men in our bed, guys that George brought home the night before.

First there's Yarrott asleep on his stomach. A hand reaches into the frame to draw the sheet off Yarrott's ass. Everyone who's seen the movie comments favorably on Yarrott's ass. He and Draper have known each other since kindergarten in Nashville. "I'm not into that," Yarrott grumbles, and rolls away from the camera, wrapping the sheet around him.

Then there's me, in close-up without my glasses, croaking sleepily that I want to be left alone. I was a last-minute replacement when a friend chickened out.

Next comes Nancy's husband, sitting up and glaring as the camera bobs toward him. Nancy is a poet who worked with me at the bookstore. Long before we began *George and Al,* she had a dream where Draper and I were shooting a movie in our apartment. "And I thought, *How practical of them.*" She didn't mind loaning us her husband, and he didn't mind playing a gay man so long as he could keep his T-shirt on. He snarls, "If you don't turn that damn thing off, I'm going to shove it up your nose."

And then comes Al. Waking to the cold, obtrusive eye of a lens, his first response is to ask, "What kind of camera is that?" Immediately, he and George seem to be made for each other.

Al is played by our good friend, John.

Where do I begin to describe John? He is such an important, complex part of our life. We met him twelve years ago, when he and Draper took an acting class at Herbert Berghof Studios. He adopted us, or maybe we adopted him—I can't remember exactly how the friendship gained momentum. He's a few years older than we are, with more lives than his two cats, Cyrano and Rimbaud, combined. He has been a teacher, a bartender, a salesclerk, and a chef. His family tree is Italian—Sicilian, to be precise. He's also an ex-monk, in and out of the Jesuits once, the Benedictines twice. As the names of his cats suggest, he's very well read. In addition, he is the only opera lover I know who can talk to agnostics without sounding like a baseball fan citing batting averages. He makes opera exciting even for me and Draper, who're hardly opera queens but, as Draper says, mere ladies-in-waiting.

Another day, another room in our apartment: the living room this time and our ruptured camelback sofa. George has invited Al over to film him secretly, shyly keeping himself out of the frame. Al spots the hidden camera, laughs, and drags George into the shot: what's good for the gander is good for the other gander. For the first time, we finally see George, or rather, Draper. It was only eight years ago, but he looks even younger, with a short curly haircut like a fox terrier. George is painfully, convincingly self-conscious. Draper dislikes performing unless he has a character to hide in, but he included bits of himself in George, gestures and simple phrases —"I'm starved"—that now seem like quotes from the movie whenever Draper uses them.

George and Al become lovers. Draper is small and John is large—he was forty pounds larger than he is now—a friendly bear with a full beard. They are not anyone's idea of a hot couple. They do make a good comedy team, however, which is probably a truer model for a longterm relationship.

George and Al have a dinner on the roof of our five-floor walk-up, with two friends played by Jennifer and Larry. Behind them is an airborne Greenwich Village landscape of low roofs and chimney pots. A few larger buildings stand above the tar-paper plain like great chests of drawers. George leaves the camera on and joins the others. (In reality, I stood at the tripod and watched everyone through the viewfinder.)

Larry is the lover of a former Episcopal minister who's one of John's best friends—gay ex-priests seem to be ecumenical.

Larry supported himself as a housepainter, but he was and is a real actor, at his best when he's pretending to be someone else. He has a barking laugh and looks like a handsome farm boy.

Jennifer goes back much further. She studied design at Pratt Institute with Draper and is another art director devoted to other arts. She loves to sing and worships Patsy Cline. She has a striking face—cheekbones, lipstick, and dark hair—and natural spontaneity. Her character keeps letting slip things George has told her that he hasn't told Al, including the fact that he's in love with Al. "This part is perfect for me," Jennifer said when she read the script. I didn't have the courage to confess that I based the character on her.

Everybody slow dances against the sunset to "Someone's Rocking My Dreamboat" by the Ink Spots. George and Al dance together. That was the contribution of my friend, Anna. We showed her some unedited footage when she was visiting from Boston, explained how it would be put together, and she said, "But we never see them being affectionate."

The affection continues into the next scene, where the lovers wordlessly dance around each other while fixing dinner in our narrow kitchen. George had wanted to film the two of them in bed, but the intimacy of cooking is the most Al will agree to expose. George's invasive mechanical eye is finally becoming a problem for Al.

Then comes the skunk party.

Ever since we saw a child in skunk pajamas at the Halloween parade one year, Draper had wanted to have a party where everyone would be dressed as skunks. Never getting to it in real life, we incorporated the scene in the movie.

You would not believe how hard it is to find a dozen people willing to dress as rodents. Draper and his friend Julia assembled the outfits: cardboard-stiffened tails, black hoods, and, for the stripe, lengths of white boa. Worn with black clothes, they were quite effective. But only a handful of friends had so little vanity they would agree to wear them.

It was one of the hottest days of July when we gathered on the roof, dressed as skunks but sweating like pigs. Nancy from the bookstore was there—this was not what she had in mind when she dreamed we'd make a movie. My cousin Maureen, who works on Wall Street, willingly offered herself—she had just come out and we'd set her up on her first date (it wasn't our fault the woman turned out to be a lunatic). Our downstairs neighbor Cook was enlisted. "This isn't a disco body," he told us, referring to his multiple sclerosis, but he was happy to stand off to the side, a sultry skunk with sideburns and a cigarette. Neighbors in surrounding buildings leaned out their windows or loitered on the fire escapes, wondering what the hell was going on. Draper shouted, "Action," and the skunks began to dance.

Jennifer and I dance on top of the hut over the door leading downstairs. I was slimmer then. Jennifer looks good even with a white stripe down her back. She was a wild, exuberant dancer, not noticing until we were done that we gyrated inches from a five-story drop down an air shaft.

"It's so Fellini!" Larry exclaims.

"Yeah. Fellini's *Bambi*," Al grumbles miserably. He agreed to the party because he thought he could have fun with George. Instead, George treats the party as a photo op, and Al as just another extra.

Al suddenly snaps, exploding at the camera. He and George get into a fight, still dressed as skunks, their argument shakily filmed from a distance by Larry. Al is sick and tired of the way George uses their life as camera fodder, and is fed up with how George always calls the shots.

Is any of this autobiographical? Yes and no. None of the truths here are literal. Like George, Draper makes movies, but he's never wanted to use us as raw material. In fact, I'm more like George than Draper is, including snippets of reality in my novels.

More important is the question of power addressed by the story: Who calls the shots in any relationship? Draper and I seem to take turns. It's how we handled *George and Al.* Writing the screenplay, I was open to suggestions, but the final decisions were mine. Directing the movie, Draper was receptive too, not just to me but to John and others. All final decisions were his, however, and he's an exacting perfectionist. John took to calling him "Erich"—in homage to Erich von Stroheim—but Draper was never cruel or manipulative. He simply had a very clear idea of how a scene should play and insisted we get it right.

After I wrote the script, my role was reduced. I operated the camera for shots where Draper appeared, but he gave detailed instructions on what to film. I occasionally played devil's advocate.

"You sure you want a medium shot here?"

"Yes! Trust me."

"I trust you. Just wondering if a long shot wouldn't—"

He gave me a look that could only be translated into the Ring Lardner phrase: " 'Shut up,' he explained."

Collaborating with a loved one has its dangers, creating whole new areas for quarrels. But arguing over which lens to use or how to pace a scene is much more interesting than arguing over more personal matters, such as why I never clean the bathroom.

In the next scene, George is in bed. With Larry. George wants to film himself having sex, and if Al won't oblige, Larry will do. Once the camera is turned on, however, George has second thoughts.

I shot this perched with the tripod on a very wobbly table. Despite what one might think, filming sex is not sexy. I was too worried about focus and exposure and sound to enjoy seeing a cute guy pluck at the waistband of his underpants. Or to be jealous that my boyfriend was beside him. Not until the film came back from the lab and Draper ran it through the projector did I catch traces of those feelings.

Our chief difficulty during the scene was a fear of giggles. It was the situation, of course, but also the dialogue. When George says he's not in the mood, Larry offers to go ahead without him. George considers it, then decides no. Larry promptly says, "All right. You want to go eat?" I burst out laughing when I wrote that line. Larry burst out laughing when he rehearsed it. Nevertheless, whenever we screen the movie, nobody has even chuckled. I assume they're too busy hoping Larry *will* masturbate.

At this point, filming on weekends and holidays, the project had gone on for six months. A new reality began to creep in. As Al grew more irritated with George, John became more annoyed with us. It wasn't method acting. He'd been very excited when we first told him about the movie and asked him to be in it, but you're asking a lot when you commit a friend to a project that goes on and on with no money involved, only friendship. The situation wasn't helped by the fact that we were a couple and John was single. John has had boyfriends in the past, but generally he's single. We were two-against-one, and a couple is a confusing animal for somebody who lives by himself: not one person, but not quite two either. We had our own little wars, resolutions, and intimacies that did not include John. And at the end of each session, no matter how well we worked together, John went home alone. He was too loyal to quit, and he continued to give his best on film, coming up with new ideas and fresh bits of business that brought a clumsy scene to life. But he became more despondent off camera.

We renewed friendship between shootings by sharing things that had nothing to do with the work in progress. John is a wonderful cook and frequently had us over for dinner. Draper and I couldn't match him there, but we duped a porn film as a Christmas present, customizing it for John by replacing the cheesy disco soundtrack with selections from Verdi. None of us can hear "Libiamo" from *La Traviata* now without thinking of bleached-blond surfers humping on the hood of a car.

We also tried matchmaking, but Draper and I are not very good at that. My friend Cedric came up for a visit from Virginia. A musician and writer, he was to provide music for the movie. I went to college with Cedric but never suspected he was gay until after we graduated and mutual friends reported the news. A gentle, longhaired chain-smoker who loved Mozart, Kafka, and Frank Zappa, Cedric seemed too original for anything so obvious as repressed sexuality. He cut his hair and shaved his beard when he came out, revealing a gentle, square-jawed face. He remained as unique as ever, though, as original as John. We thought they might hit it off. Alas, they were too original for each other, and too similar, both of them smart and tall and locked in private dreams of what they wanted in a boyfriend. While he stayed with us, Cedric kept apologizing for the repeated trips he made to Gay Treasures, a nearby store that sells old pornography, to stock up on magazines that didn't exist back home.

After George sleeps with Larry, he and Al continue to see each other, although Al refuses to let George film him anymore. George films him on the sly one day, following Al to his job and around town. There's a sad, wrongheaded desperation in George's stolen glimpses of Al. The shots of Manhattan from the summer of 1986 look oddly historical now.

Then comes the scene that's the heart of the movie. Using George's camera as an answering machine, Al leaves a message. His soulful, rumpled face filling the frame, Al explains what he feels about George, and about his camera. "When you film me I feel like an object. When I film you I feel like a servant. We have to find a way to work this out."

And they do. Their solution is to invent a fantasy together, their own fictional movie, a short Charlie Chaplin parody.

When Draper and I first met, one of the things that tightened our bond was a love of silent movies. German expressionism, Soviet epic, American melodrama: we enjoyed them all. But we had a special affection for Charlie Chaplin. We knew his work thoroughly, from the early shorts through *The Kid* to *City Lights*. And Draper could do an uncanny Chaplin impersonation. He not only looked like Chaplin in makeup and costume, he could catch the inventive spirit of him, the coyness, pathos, grace, and malice. One of our bedtime stories had been to imagine a gay Chaplin film—the Little Tramp is so polymorphous that it's not much of a stretch. John made a perfect Chaplin partner, the larger foils played by Mack Swain, Eric Campbell, and others. Just as we found a use for our skunk party, we found a place here for Charlie Chaplin. The movie is a scrapbook of shared fantasies.

Iris-out on our roof again, this time in black-and-white. Mack Swain and Chaplin are roofers. Chaplin is in love with Swain, who cares only about his work. Chaplin bats his eyes and dreams of bliss—and is hit on the head by the roll of tar paper swung around by Swain. During lunch, Swain in baggy clothes and droopy moustache sits down to devour a loaf of bread stuffed with sausages. Unable to take his eyes off his beloved, Chaplin mistakes a pot of glue for mustard and daintily spreads some on his own little sandwich. He tastes it, shudders, sniffs the sandwich, then sniffs the pot. He tosses the sandwich aside to happily inhale the glue. He jumps up for a wild dance of leaps and poses and pirouettes—Draper's mother taught ballet—and hops up on the parapet, thinking he can fly. Terrified for his pal, Swain climbs up to coax him back to safety. Glancing down at the five-story drop, Swain gasps and slips. He clings to the bricks for a moment, then falls. Chaplin screams for help, pinches his nose, and, as if his beloved has fallen overboard, jumps in to save him. The bodies drop together. Blackout. And Chaplin comes to, in Swain's arms. They're still on the roof, their fall a glue-sniffer's hallucination. Iris-in on Chaplin and Swain's embrace. The end, of the movie-within-the-movie, and the movie itself.

It's a terrific sequence. I knew it was good when I wrote it. I'd originally intended for George and Al to break up, split apart by the camera. But when this slapstick love-death unexpectedly came to me, I felt that two guys who made anything so weird and wonderful had to stay together.

What was a joy to write, however, was a dog to shoot. I thought I made our work easier by setting the sequence on our roof. Draper wanted it to have the even, shadowless light of silent film, which was achieved by shooting under gauzy tents of muslin. We found we could get the same effect by filming on overcast days. But cloudy skies sometimes clear up and sometimes rain. Day after day, Draper and John put on their costumes, clown-white makeup and black eyeshadow, then sat grumpily in our living room waiting for the weather to change. Months later, on rainless overcast mornings, Draper or I still said to each other, "Looks like a good day for Chaplin and Swain."

Weekend after weekend, we climbed up to the roof and shot the damn scene. Take after take. It's surprisingly difficult to achieve such standard shtick as the head repeatedly ducking in time to miss being hit by a swinging object. But bit by bit, we put it together.

The project had gone on so long now that I became John's ally in impatience. I'd finally sold my first novel and was busy with rewrites, but Draper expected me to put my work aside whenever he needed a cameraman. I was not in a generous state of mind the afternoon we threw George and Al off the roof.

Using Styrofoam heads and clothes stuffed with newspaper and weighted with old shoes, Draper and Julia built lifelike dummies of Chaplin and Swain. Jennifer told us we could use her roof for the drop—there was too much traffic on our street and we didn't want to give an innocent passerby a stroke—but she had to work that Saturday. John too said he was busy. So it was just Draper, me, and the dummies. We lugged the figures out to the street and hailed a cab. It was the morning after another Halloween parade and the driver gave us only the briefest of jaded looks.

We hauled the dummies up to Jennifer's roof and Draper went down to the street to set up the camera. I waited for his signal, wanting to get this over with. I had to keep myself hidden behind the wall so "Erich" would have no reason to complain. I rolled the Swain dummy over the edge. I couldn't watch its fall. Only when I heard it hit the ground did I begin to sense anything strange here. I tossed the Chaplin dummy and, as the figure left my hands, it suddenly wasn't just Chaplin but Draper in effigy. My heart jumped into my throat. I heard a heavy thud and thump, and my heart broke.

"Cut!" Draper shouted from the street.

I timidly looked over the edge, a guilty emotional wreck when I saw the twisted Chaplin on the pavement.

I was kinder to Draper over the next few days.

The filming was over but the movie wasn't finished. It still had to be edited, the soundtrack mixed, and music added. Draper spent the next weeks bent over the editor as if at a sewing machine, contentedly lost in his work. He involved yet another friend for the sound, Chad, a sweet-tempered audio wonk who lived in our building's basement with his girlfriend, the super, before they broke up. Chad had been helping all along, sharing advice and microphones. Cedric returned to town to record the music.

I was present the afternoon they taped the score in a cluttered little studio off Times Square. Cedric played the piano while watching Chaplin and Swain on a video monitor. Usually so laid-back and dreamy, Cedric grimaced over the keyboard, twisting his body and juggling his hands, frantically improvising phrases that brought out details, stitched them together and made a brilliant piece of music in itself. Even the technicians were impressed. When he finished, he took a deep breath, sat back, and resumed his sheepish, self-deprecating calm.

It's hard to say when *George and Al* was finally done. If it had been commercially released or shown at a major film festival, that might make a good end to the story. But nothing ever came of our movie. Too short to be a feature, too long to be used as filler, too experimental for television, and too narrative to qualify for the New Queer Cinema that came into being a few years later, our creation never found a home. Which is sad considering how much work we put into it. Draper had been protectively realistic from the start, quipping that it might lead to a career for him as a Chaplin impersonator, available for shopping mall openings and children's parties.

There was no gala screening for the cast and crew. The closest we came was the night we showed it to John. He hadn't wanted to watch himself until the thing was completed. We met at Chad's studio. Jennifer was there, although she'd already watched her scenes. We didn't bother to dim the lights, only pulled a few chairs around the monitor.

Seeing a worked and reworked movie with someone who's seeing it for the first time forces you to watch with fresh eyes. I discovered that night that it was a real movie. I couldn't tell if it was good or bad, but it was funny, dramatic, and unpredictable, with a life independent of the people who made it.

When it was over, I was pleased, Jennifer ecstatic, Chad and Draper satisfied. John, however, sat very quiet, very still. He remained quiet while everyone praised his performance. He complimented Draper on a job well done and went home.

Over the following week, meeting first with me and then with both of us, John discussed what he felt, a mix of admiration and deep disappointment. He liked the movie, was impressed Draper had pulled it off, but—and he said it first as a joke—he couldn't help feeling that what had been his show was stolen at the end by Charlie Chaplin.

He hated saying that. We had always talked about it as *our* movie. John apologized for what he felt; Draper and I tried to assure him it was his movie too. But there was a grain of truth in what he said—people who see *George and Al* usually begin by praising Draper's Chaplin—although Draper never intended to steal the show, and it's not like anyone gained anything in the end except experience.

A few months later, we were all reduced to supporting players when John left a videocassette with an agent at William Morris and the man's only response was, "I know somebody who'd love to meet the blond with the nice ass."

Looking back on it now, I see there was more than injured pride in John's dissatisfaction. It had none of the egotism of an upstaged actor. He never mentioned—didn't even seem to notice—how good he is in the movie. Acting is an odd business, a slightly masochistic art where people offer up their faces, bodies, voices, their very selves, as raw ingredients. Even the most experienced actors dislike watching their performances, and John was new to acting. His personality was too rich and deep for him to step out and blithely regard himself from afar, or to split an expendable performing self from his real self, which is what veteran actors seem to do. Maybe that was another cause for his growing unhappiness while we shot: he was defenseless. John had offered us a piece of real self and then, when he found the experience more disturbing than he expected, was too generous to take it back until the movie was finished.

Part of the appeal of filmmaking is the attraction of working with others, a sociable creativity instead of our usual artistic solitude. The Italian director, Ermanno Olmi, called it "This idea of making films around a table together, not just to live, to eat, but to look into each other's eyes." That, of course, is a director talking. Other people at the table will have a different opinion. But the idea retains its appeal, even now when I know the dangers of mixing the personal with this mechanical art. We looked into each other's eyes for several months— Draper, John, and I and the rest—saw things we hadn't seen before, and continued, changed in great ways and small.

When I watch *George and Al* now, it's a photo album of a past that remains connected to the present.

Since then, Draper has made three more short films, each better than the last. He no longer needs his boyfriend behind the camera, but works with professionals, which is fine by me. I remain involved from outside, offering ideas, screenplays, and a sympathetic ear.

Meanwhile, Jennifer bought a video camera and is interviewing women for her own documentary. Chad handles the sound for trade shows, continues to work with Draper, and has a girlfriend who's a first-rate theater director. Nancy and her husband moved to Seattle. Cedric finally moved to New York, where he plays piano for dance classes. Larry appeared briefly on Broadway in an evening of Thornton Wilder one-acts. And John, despite *George and Al,* continued to act. He performed with Karen Allen in an off-Broadway production of *The Miracle Worker* and began to work as a movie extra. He put acting aside three years ago, saying only that he did not have time for it since he opened his catering business. But that's him in *Prizzi's Honor,* holding the bag of silver-plated golf clubs at the Mafia banquet. John Huston, in his rolling, mouthful-of-plums voice, told the cameraman, "And be sure you get this man's face. He has such a marvelous face."

1995

HOMAGE TO
MR. JIMMY

—◠◡◠—

P EOPLE OF MY generation first encountered his movies on the Friday night late
show: *Frankenstein*, *Bride of Frankenstein*, *The
Invisible Man*, *The Old Dark House*. We were
kids and it was past our bedtime, so these
movies were like dreams—dark, disturbing, wonderful dreams we could share with
friends. There were other horror movies
too—*Dracula*, *The Wolfman*, *The Creature from
the Black Lagoon*—but even then many of us
knew that the first set of titles were better,
classier, somehow funnier *and* scarier. Not

until we were older did we notice that they'd all been made by the same man, a director named James Whale.

I went to college in Virginia in the 1970s, which was a golden age of cinema, foreign and American. I fell in love with movies. I thought of myself as a would-be director long before I became a would-be novelist. I was a movie snob for a long time, turning up my nose at old Hollywood, avoiding the monster flicks until I was well into my thirties. I was living in New York with Draper, another movie junkie (we were already making short films together), when one winter the local PBS station showed all the horror classics. That's when I truly discovered Whale.

His movies were a revelation. First there was their look. They were playfully stylish, mixing expressionist camera angles, elegant long shots, and manic, silent movie editing. The emotions were oddly sophisticated. *Frankenstein*, his first horror picture, is almost classical in its feeling, yet with surprising sympathy for the monster. In the next films, however, Whale began to mix things up. *The Invisible Man* and especially *The Old Dark House* are black comedies. *The Bride of Frankenstein* is blacker still, and marvelously slippery, leaping from horror to comedy to pathos to parody. Whale was playing games of genre-fuck long before Billy Wilder and François Truffaut.

Whale made other movies beside the horror films. His *Show Boat* remains one of the best screen adaptations of an American stage musical. His version of *Waterloo Bridge* is a perfect little melodrama, *By Candlelight* a deft little comedy in the style of Ernst Lubitsch. But the monster movies were different; the monster movies were new. There was nothing quite like them when they first came along. They are where Whale made his mark on cinema history. I sincerely believe *Bride of Frankenstein* is one of the great American films, right up there with *Citizen Kane, Sunset Boulevard,* and *Godfather II.*

Around the time I rediscovered the horror movies, I learned that Whale was gay. A gay man myself, I couldn't help being intrigued. Vito Russo in his groundbreaking book, *The Celluloid Closet,* repeated the rumor that Whale's career ended in 1941 because he was too open about his sexuality. There was also the mystery of his death: he was found drowned in his swimming pool in 1957. I read conflicting reports of accident, suicide or murder. And then, one night over dinner, a British friend, a documentary filmmaker, told me something I hadn't heard yet: Whale had fought in the First World War; he was a working-class boy who'd served in the trenches. Which gave a whole new dimension to the man. The horror movies weren't just spooky kids' stuff anymore, but war stories, pieces of auto-biography. I became utterly fascinated with Whale that night. I couldn't stop thinking about him.

I didn't know what to do with my obsession. I'm a novelist, not a biographer or I would've written a biography. I began to make notes for something, maybe a screenplay, about the last weeks of Whale's life. "I don't know," said Draper. "Sounds like a novel to me."

Reading around, I found there wasn't much about Whale, and a lot of it was clearly make-believe. Then I stumbled on a small book published by Scarecrow Press in 1982, *James Whale* by James Curtis. It was a gold mine. I didn't always agree with Curtis's interpretations (I agreed even less when he expanded the book for a new edition in 1998), but his facts always rang true. When Curtis didn't have a fact, he was silent, which might be maddening for the general reader but gave my imagination more room to work in. A few facts go a long way in fiction. You don't need or even want to know everything. There's a fine movie by the Swiss filmmaker Alain Tanner, *La Salamandre*, where two friends, a novelist and a journalist, research a murder. The journalist uses facts; the novelist uses narrative logic. At one point the novelist insists, "No more facts! They only get in my way!" The two men arrive at more or less the same solution.

The Curtis book gave me something else I needed: it solved the mystery of Whale's death. Debilitated by a stroke, aware he would never get better, he took his own life. Curtis published the suicide note that Whale's well-meaning ex-lover, David Lewis, hid for twenty-four years. This carefully chosen death seemed fitting for a man whose monster famously said, "Love dead, hate living."

My original intention was to write a hybrid of biography and fiction, one of those meta-novels where the novelist regularly pokes his head through the backdrop to tell the reader what's real and what's made up. It was my overly scrupulous way of writing fiction about a real man. Then I hit upon the character of Clay Boone, who is entirely fictional. Clay was going to be minor figure, an occasional visitor whom the general reader could identify with. But Clay took on a life of his own; the dangerous friendship between him and Whale grew and deepened and became the center of the novel. I took out the pesky authorial commentary: it had eased me into the story but now only got in the way. The story had its own momentum and I stopped worrying about historical truth. As I neared the ending, I actually began to resent history. One day I confessed to my agent that I was feeling frustrated. "No matter what I invent for Whale, he still has end up dead at the bottom of that damned swimming pool." My agent laughed and said, "Quit grousing. Most authors don't know how their novels end, and you've been handed a great ending."

I finished a first draft and showed it to a few trusted readers. I learned what worked and what didn't, then wrote a new draft. My agent sent the novel out. There were rejections, some politer than others, until Matthew Carnicelli at Dutton took it. He loved the book, but wondered if I might put more Hollywood in, just to juice it up for the general reader. I resisted, until my friend Ed Sikov read it. Ed is a film historian and I only wanted him to catch my errors. Ed found the history accurate, but he too wanted more Hollywood. "Not for juice," he said, "but because I want to know more about Whale's life when he was successful." *Of course.* I went back and wrote two new flashback scenes, including the premiere of *Camille* where Whale meets Garbo, one of my favorite chapters.

The book was published in 1995 as *Father of Frankenstein* to good reviews and decent sales. I began to hear from other people who knew and loved Whale's movies. There's a huge world of monster fans out there and some are very smart. I became good friends with one, David Skal, author of an excellent cultural history of horror, *The Monster Show.* David had arrived factually at some of the very ideas that I discovered imaginatively, in particular the role of the First World War in the horror films. Whale incorporated not only the horror of the trenches, but its gallows humor, which he mixed with the bitter gay sarcasm that is part of "camp." The monster movies opened the door on a new twentieth-century sensibility that drew upon humor, history, and sexuality.

I also heard from people who'd known my protagonist. There was a letter from the niece of David Lewis, the ex-lover: she understood I was writing fiction but was sorry I'd made her uncle bald. She told me politely but firmly that he died with a full head of hair. Yet I failed Lewis in another, more important way, which I heard about from other people, including the writer Gavin Lambert. Lewis was not closeted but fairly open about being gay. When he worked at Warner Brothers, before he and Whale broke up, Jack Warner called him into his office one day and said, "Do you have to live with Mr. Whale?" "I don't *have* to live with him," said Lewis. "I *want* to live with him." I'd misread between the lines in an account about Lewis, but my mistake wasn't just factual. For the sake of the story, I needed a gay man who was more guarded than Whale, more representative of their time. Lewis was my fall guy. You should also remember we see Lewis only from Whale's point of view, and exes aren't always objective. Nevertheless, David Lewis was a richer, more complex, bolder man than the figure in the novel.

But you probably want to hear about the movie, don't you? Everyone enjoys hearing about the movie, and I don't blame them, especially since it turned out so well. Novelists are supposed to hate the films made from their books, but I love mine.

I never think in terms of a future movie while writing a

novel, not even this one. However, shortly after finishing *Father*, I saw the film of *Six Degrees of Separation* with Stockard Channing and Donald Sutherland. In the part of a charming friend was the great British actor, Sir Ian McKellen. Afterward I told Draper, "McKellen would make a great Whale. He even looks a little like him." I mentioned this to my agent, who not only agreed but knew McKellen's address. We sent him an advance copy with a note: "If this were ever made into a movie . . ." I got a nice note back. "I'm terribly busy with *Richard III* right now but look forward to reading your book one day." I figured that was be the end of it.

Over the next months, before the novel came out, a couple of major studios asked to see it. My agent and I were pleasantly surprised. This interest promptly disappeared after the new Tim Burton movie, *Ed Wood*, opened to great reviews and bad box office. They must have thought movies about weird old directors were the next new thing and wanted to be ready with one of their own. Their curiosity didn't last long enough for me to get a lunch out of it.

Finally, the book was published and I heard from my agent again. A young director wanted to option it for a possible low-budget independent feature. "His name is Bill Condon. His last film was *Candyman II*. Shall we pursue this?"

Well, beggars can't be choosers. Some wonderful directors started out making B-pictures, although at this point, to be honest, I just wanted the option money.

Only after the contract was signed did Bill and I talk on the phone. And we liked each other instantly. He too loved movies, all kinds. He loved Whale's work and understood how the horror films were simultaneously funny and profound. And we had friends in common, including Ed Sikov. I told Bill the book was his baby now, but he was free to pick my brain. He said there were a few changes he was considering, including making the housekeeper, Maria, Central European rather than Mexican American. "Go ahead," I told him. "I realized in the middle of writing the book that she's based on my Swiss-German grandmother." He also wanted to try something different for the ending. I told him about an epilogue I couldn't make work, where Clay is married with two kids and he wakes his son one night to watch *Bride of Frankenstein* on the late show. "Hmm," said Bill. "Do you mind if I try something like that?" He asked if I had any ideas for actors to play Whale. I told him how I'd sent the bound galleys to McKellen. "Ian McKellen, huh? Hmm."

Bill wrote the screenplay that summer and showed me the first draft. He listened to my good suggestions and ignored my bad ones, but the truth is we saw things the same way ninety percent of the time. He kept me posted on what was happening with money and casting. Clive Barker came on as executive producer; his chief contribution was the use of his name and the loan of a nice house where Bill could meet Sir Ian. When Ian first read the script, he said no, it was a gay suicide story. "With my politics, I can't play such a role." "Please read it again," said Bill. "You'll see something else is there." Ian did and liked what he saw and he committed to the project. He was good friends with Lynn Redgrave; they'd always wanted to work together, so Lynn came on as the housekeeper, now renamed and renationalized.

A very talented, up-and-coming actor named Brendan Fraser was approached for the part of Clay. He liked the script but didn't like the title. He thought *Father of Frankenstein* sounded like a cheesy horror picture, which is the point, of course, but Bill couldn't bring him around. My theory is that after starring in *Airheads* and *George of the Jungle,* Brendan felt that if he were going to do a serious movie, it damn well better have a serious title. Since his involvement meant that Showtime would put up a million dollars, what Brendan wanted Brendan got. "What do you think of *Gods and Monsters* for a title?" asked Bill apologetically. "The only other one I can think of is *Mr. Jimmy*"—the housekeeper's name for Whale. "No, *Gods and Monsters* is better," I agreed. (There was talk of changing the title back, but it didn't happen. Since the movie is now better known, it's easier to rename the novel, which I'm happy to do, not least because the novel's title has become *Father-of-Frankenstein-basis-for-the-movie-Gods-and-Monsters.* The new title is shorter.)

Filming began in July 1997, a little more than two years after my first talk with Bill—virtually overnight in Hollywood time. There was a twenty-one-day shooting schedule and a budget of only three and a half million dollars. Draper and I flew out to Los Angeles toward the end of the shoot. We arrived one afternoon at Occidental Studios, an old soundstage from the 1930s, and walked into the vast empty set for *Bride of Frankenstein.* "My God," I said. "I write one little paragraph and look at all the work somebody had to do."

"You're the novelist?" a nervous production assistant asked. "Does Bill know *the writer* is here?" We assured him that Bill had invited us.

We hung out for three days, talking to Ian, Brendan, and Rosalind Ayres, who plays Elsa Lanchester, the monster's bride. (Lynn Redgrave had already finished her scenes and I didn't meet her for another five years. "You were channeling my grandmother and didn't know it," I told her. "My family is thrilled.") Ian didn't remember getting an advance copy of the novel. "Did I write back? Oh good. I read your novel, but only after I read the script. You see, one is sent so many things that I read nothing unless there's money attached." Then he added, "But a friend read the book when it came out and he told me, 'There's a nice part for you if this ever becomes a movie.'" Brendan was terribly earnest, telling me he'd read the novel three times and asking if Clay were named Clay as an allusion to the subtitle of Mary Shelley's *Frankenstein*: "A Modern Prometheus." He said, "Prometheus makes a man out of clay. James Whale makes a man out of Clay Boone." "Uh, yeah, that works," I said. "But to be honest, I just wanted a good white trash name."

Also on the set was David Skal, who was making a behind-the-scenes documentary. The shoot felt like a party, a joyful meeting of the Friends of James Whale.

Two months later, back in New York, Draper and I sat in our living room and watched a video rough cut of the movie. It was one of the strangest experiences of my life. This was something that was mine yet not mine. I'd read the script and seen the actors, but I had never guessed how close the landscape on the screen would be to the landscape in my head.

"That must've been weird for you," said Draper afterward. "Like hearing somebody retell the dream you had the night before."

"Oh yeah," I said. "Only I can't get over how close the telling is to my dream. Is it any good?"

Because I couldn't tell. The movie *is* true to the novel, and the artist has no distance from his work. I could see it was well done. All through it are bits of business added by the actors or director that are so good I couldn't help thinking, "Why didn't I do that?" And yet, it *is* my story. I couldn't tell if it worked or not. Only when I began to watch the film with other people, first the rough cut on video with friends, then the finished print in theaters full of strangers, could I see that it actually was good. Which means the book is good. Doesn't it? Believe it or not, one is never sure.

Books and movies are often discussed as if they were enemies, with the implication that visual cultural is destroying literature, and literature is superior. But bad books are as common as bad movies. It's true that a movie can drive a book out of your head, even a book you wrote yourself. Movies are so strong visually, the physical presence of actors more solid than anything that can be conjured with words alone. And yet, as Jean Renoir said, "A movie is such a little thing." Only so much can be packed into a hour or two of screen time, and it's all surface. Good as the movie of *Gods and Monsters* is, there are huge swatches of the novel that were left out, whole realms of interior life and past history that only get hinted at. A movie must concentrate experience, like a dream, while a novel is more like waking life, full of prose as well as poetry.

I love novels and I love movies. I like to think that the book and the film of *Gods and Monsters* complete each other. Most readers of a book make a movie in their own head anyway;

some movie-makers are better than others, but it's the risk all novelists take. We put ourselves in your hands. I was in excellent hands with Bill Condon and his amazing cast and crew. I find I'm usually in good hands with readers, too.

Gods and Monsters opened in November 1998. The reviews were terrific and the distributor, Lions Gate, knew how to find an audience, starting the film in Los Angeles and New York, then slowly opening it wider. Bill took to referring to it as "the little movie that could." In February, Oscar nominations were announced. *Gods and Monsters* was nominated for three: Ian McKellen for Best Actor, Lynn Redgrave for Best Supporting Actress, and Bill Condon for Best Screenplay Adapted from Another Source. We all assumed I'd attend the ceremony with Bill, until we found out that tickets were limited and Lions Gate had scarfed up all the extras. I was actually relieved: I didn't have to worry about renting a tux.

On Oscar night I was in Virginia, where I was writer-in-residence that semester at the College of William and Mary, my old alma mater. I invited a few friends and a couple of students over to watch the show. The "buzz" was that *Gods and Monsters* would lose in all three categories. As the evening progressed, the predictions appeared to be accurate. Lynn lost to Judi Dench in *Shakespeare in Love.* Ian lost to Roberto Benigni in *Life Is Beautiful*—the sight of Benigni leaping seats like a monkey is unhappily burned into my brain. It was getting late and my guests began to leave.

Finally, the screenwriting nominees were read out by Goldie Hawn and Steve Martin. "And the winner is," said Goldie Hawn, "Bill Condon for *Gods and Monsters.*"

There was silence in my living room for three long seconds. Then we all jumped up and began to yell.

Bill raced up on stage to accept the award. "First I have to thank Chris Bram who wrote *Father of Frankenstein*. This is a very faithful adaptation." Down in the audience, Ian, Lynn and Brendan arranged themselves into a trio of beaming faces for the TV camera.

And my phone rang. It was Draper back home in New York, watching in an apartment full of noisy friends.

Bill continued to thank people until he closed by thanking Whale himself. "Sixty years ago, Hollywood sort of turned its back on him because he insisted on living the way he wanted. So, Mr. Jimmy," he said, lifting the Oscar at the camera—I later held it myself and it's remarkably heavy. "This is for you."

2005

GLASS
CLOSET

—∿—

HE WAS THE little Frenchman with Charlie
Chaplin eyes who, so the story goes,
dipped some cake in his tea one day, had a
vision, and shut himself in a cork-lined room
to write a seven-volume novel about it. But
A la recherche du temps perdu, or *Remembrance of
Things Past,* or *In Search of Lost Time*—whatever
one wants to call Marcel Proust's life work
(forced to choose between pretension or
inaccuracy, most people simply say, "I'm reading Proust")—is one of the glories of literature, an introverted epic about childhood,

love, *belle époque* Paris, and the value of art. It's also one of the funniest novels ever written, and nobody ever created better party scenes.

Considering how few people actually read his 3,000-page masterpiece, Proust has been the subject of a remarkable number of excellent short books. I think the two phenomena are related: when you fall in love with Proust and find nobody with whom you can discuss his magic, you have no choice except to write another book.

There are fine book-length essays by Samuel Beckett, Howard Moss, and J. M. Cocking, a wonderful introductory study by Roger Shattuck in the old Modern Masters series, and, most recently, Alain de Botton's deceptively entertaining, subtly wise, *How Proust Can Change Your Life*. Now Edmund White packs Proust's life into a concise, solid, highly readable work of 150 pages.

Marcel Proust is the first in a new series, Penguin Lives, of short, personal biographies by novelists and critics. White and Proust are an excellent match. Both men combine lyrical sensibility with analytic intellect, White is a dedicated Francophile, and his autobiographical trilogy—*A Boy's Own Story, The Beautiful Room Is Empty,* and *The Farewell Symphony*—walks alongside Proust's elaborate footsteps.

There is little of the rhapsodic White here, however. This is a work of literary scholarship, the language quick and sharp, White's word-painting showing itself only in occasional flourishes such as a description of the family apartment in Paris or sketches of the streets where Proust lived. White keeps himself out of the picture in order to pack in details and rapid takes on different aspects of the man's life: his social circles; his Jewish heritage (on his mother's side); his curious households; his life in art.

Where White's point of view does show, and to good effect, is in his treatment of Proust's homosexuality. He is refreshingly matter-of-fact about it, without any of the judgmental weirdness one finds in George Painter's famous two-volume biography (Painter claimed Proust was a bisexual who renounced his heterosexuality out of a failure of self-esteem, or some such nonsense), and none of the anachronistic scolding of gay readers annoyed by the shell game that Proust played with his sexuality.

Proust made his autobiographical narrator straight, but then his imagination took its revenge by giving almost everyone else in his novel a queer streak. He denounced homosexuality in a famous essay-like chapter, then gave the first full, unembarrassed account of a gay demimonde, with one character, the Baron de Charlus, who transcends all judgments, one of the finest creations in literature. In life Proust was just as divided and unpredictable, breaking off with friends who called him unmanly, even fighting a few duels, while telling others his vice was quite common and part of his wisdom. He told his housekeeper he went to male brothels, but only for research. He was a closet case, but one who lived in a glass closet, and at a time when homosexuality destroyed reputations. White treats this with understanding and sympathy. His Proust is sometimes dark, even pathological, but always recognizably human, never freakish.

White is also good on his career, the seriousness with

which this apparent dilettante took his vocation, the false starts and unfinished projects that eventually led him to one mammoth book. There are no new discoveries here, but White presents the chronology with more clarity than any other account I've read.

His reading of the novel itself is clear and lucid, although de Botton does a better job of making a neophyte want to plunge into that vast, beautiful country. White makes a good case for the Albertine volumes being necessary to the dramatic structure of the whole, without admitting that those pages and pages of split hairs can be like crossing the Mojave Desert for even the most smitten reader. He takes involuntary memory a bit more literally than I do—I consider it a brilliant storytelling device, much like "Rosebud" in *Citizen Kane*, rather than an important psychological truth—but is very good on Proust as a philosopher, and wonderful on his treatment of character, which he rightly says combine the vividness of Dickens with the depth and shading of Henry James.

All in all, this is a fine book, an excellent introduction to Proust the man. It should intrigue more people into tackling the novel. Because that is ultimately what any book about Proust aims for: to make you read the thing itself. And the novel is daunting. It can require as many false starts by the reader as the author needed to write it. My advice is to pick up *Swann's Way*, the first volume, which is sort of a Proust sampler, offering all his different voices. If you bog down after a hundred pages or so of "Combray," the childhood chapter, skip ahead to "Swann in Love," which is like a short novel tucked inside the long one. "Swann in Love" should win your trust and enable you to continue. Trust and patience are the two qualities any reader of Proust needs. Because everything adds up, if you give it time. These seven volumes can change the way you look at life, like a pair of magic bifocals that enable you to see both deep into yourself and far out into the world.

1999

CAN STRAIGHT MEN
STILL WRITE?

—⁓—

I AM A PROMISCUOUS reader of fiction. I'll read anyone who has a good story to tell: male, female, gay, straight, American, British, Israeli, or Czech. As a gay man, I'll often finish a mediocre novel with gay content that I might drop otherwise, but the best novels can turn me happily pansexual. I don't read with an agenda, but simply follow my nose, taking up whatever catches my curiosity, wanting to get as much fictional life as I can.

Nevertheless, a few years ago I discovered a peculiar blind spot in my reading. Putting together a box of books to take with me for a month in the woods, an accumulation of recent titles by favorite authors— Nadine Gordimer, Milan Kundera, Anne Tyler, Edmund White, A. B. Yehoshua—I found that I had no new novels by straight American men. I seemed to have stopped reading them.

It was not a conscious decision. I have no prejudice against Dead White Males, or live ones either. I had never been an "affirmative action" reader. Now, however, out of a fair-mindedness that might be called political correctness, I worked to correct my blind spot, asking well-read friends to recommend new novels by straight men. But they too reported that their favorite recent books were all by women, gay men, or foreigners. Even my agent's assistant, a young straight male, had noticed a similar shift in his reading for pleasure, although he then recommended *Mohawk* by Richard Russo, which I thoroughly enjoyed—an upstate New York *Last Picture Show* for grown-ups—but it seemed an exception that proved the rule.

Since then, I've made a point of occasionally reading novels by straight men, and continue to find exceptions. No, I don't read everything, and my evidence is hardly conclusive. Yet the heterosexual men who move me remain startlingly few. Russell Banks is one. His deceptively simple novel, *The Sweet Hereafter*, about the aftermath of a school bus wreck in a small town, explores a tangle of public event and personal need with a moral complexity that shows up Tom Wolfe's *Bonfire of the Vanities* for the smug cartoon it really is. Lewis Nordan in *Wolf Whistle* wraps the voice of Southern comedy around the Emmett Till murder for a shocking novel where comic, recognizably human characters are capable of a sickening crime.

More recently, I read *Men in Black* by Scott Spencer, a risky book that mixes cultural satire with embarrassingly real private emotions, the most nakedly honest novel about a good married man who can sometimes be a shit since, well, a short novel by a woman, Jane Smiley's *The Age of Grief.* Such spot judgments are very personal, of course, but then reading is a highly subjective act. I can only report my own experience. I often find the surprise and truth that I expect of good writing in nonfiction by straight men—Neil Sheehan, Lawrence Weschler, Henry Louis Gates Jr., and others—and in fiction by men of an earlier generation—the late Wallace Stegner. But I am regularly disappointed, if not downright bored, by the current celebrated names of straight male fiction.

How strange that phrase sounds: straight male fiction. But after years of talking about women's fiction, gay fiction, and lesbian fiction, why not talk about that other species?

I don't mean to say, "Straight men bad, everyone else good." What I'm trying to identify and understand is a dead style of thinking about literary fiction that many straight men, and the reputation machine, still cling to.

The recent critical triumph of Richard Ford, for example, baffles me. I read *The Sportswriter* years ago, liked the sharp prose, but lost patience with the narrator's "I'm all right, Jack" act over the death of his son, end of his marriage, and suicide of a friend. Frank Bascomb's emotional lockjaw, meant to suggest grace under pressure, gave unearned importance to emotions that were never expressed or examined. In the prize-winning sequel, *Independence Day,* Frank has dropped sports writing to sell real estate. He's still playing suburban philosopher, only he no longer speaks in clean, clipped sentences but a windy, smartass, evasive voice. The novel is Frank's hour-by-hour account of a Fourth of July weekend when he tries to sell a house, copes with a semi-girlfriend, and takes his surviving son, a generically alienated fourteen-year-old, to the Baseball Hall of Fame. Too much is made of the minor irony that a man who sells homes has no real home of his own, but what ultimately kills the book for me is its flabbiness, unconvincing details, and Frank's windbag wisdom.

> The truth is—and this may be my faith in progress talking— my old Hoving Road house looks more like a funeral home now than it looks like my house or a house where any past of mine took place. And this odd feeling I have is of having passed on (not in the bad way) to a recognition that ghosts ascribed to places where you once were only confuse matters with their intractable lack of corroborating substance. I frankly think that if I sat here in my car five more minutes, staring out at my old house like a visitant to an oracle's flame, I'd find that what felt like melancholy was just a prelude to bursting out laughing and needlessly freezing a sweet small piece of my heart I'd be better off to keep than lose.

The book is full of this stuff, Frank treating his almost-felt emotions like gold. After two novels totaling seven hundred-plus pages, anal-retentive epiphanies get awfully old.

A far better writer is Tim O'Brien, especially when he writes on Vietnam and evokes the slow-motion horror that drives his young soldiers into fantasy or callousness. Nevertheless, I needed more from his ambitious, ingeniously structured novel about a Vietnam vet politician, *In the Lake of the Woods*, than a coy, metafictional tapdance around a murdered wife. It's a multiple-choice novel where the reader can choose other scenarios, none very plausible, but which together disguise the rote, mechanical nature of the violence at the book's center.

Cormac McCarthy in *All the Pretty Horses* drops his usual opaque, clotted prose, like bad Faulkner left on the stove too long, for a stripped-out version of good Faulkner, producing a tight, well-structured novel like a black-and-white Western from the sixties. There's a nice touch of *Waiting for Godot* in the laconic exchanges between two teenage cowboys who travel down to Mexico. Despite a clumsy romantic interlude, it's a pleasant enough performance, but with no real depth or power. It's hard to see what the hoopla was about. With his next novel, *The Crossing*, McCarthy returned to his old inexpressive, overcooked verbiage.

But the prose is rarely what's wrong with these books. Good prose in new novels is as common as good photography in recent movies, and often wonderful in itself. Look at Nicholson Baker. A gifted, original stylist, Baker is a miniaturist, a detail freak whose driving urge is to duplicate the minutiae of contemporary life. He's often compared to Nabokov, although his looping digressions also remind me of Laurence Sterne, with the important difference that Baker keeps his books short so they don't grow tiresome the way *Tristram Shandy* does. *Vox* consists entirely of a long phone conversation between two detail freaks, a man and woman who meet on a sex line. The inevitable outcome of their chat is delayed with a string of wonderful digressions about underwear, pornography, and stereo equipment, and the woman's account of a trip to the circus:

> Anyhow for the big finale she rode around on this elephant's tusks for a minute or two, sat on his trunk, fine, fine, all gracefully executed but surprisingly suggestive, and then she did this thing that really shocked me. She took hold of one of the ears and one of the tusks, or somehow swung herself up and then lifted one of her knees so it went right into the elephant's mouth, and she waited a second for the elephant to clamp on to it, and then she threw her head back and arched her back and spread her arms wide, so she was held in the air supported entirely by her knee, which was stuffed in the elephant's mouth! I mean, think about the saliva! Think about those elephant molars that are gently but firmly taking hold of your upper calf and your mid-thigh, while this elephant tongue is there lounging with its giant taste-buds against your knee!

Allan Gurganus uses a similar bait-and-tease in his earlier short story "Adult Art," from *White People*, where the suspense of a gay sexual pursuit is prolonged by digressions into the lives of two men, a happily married school superintendent and a nerdy loner. I don't know if "Adult Art" influenced Baker (he's one of the few straight men who actually reads and admires gay writers), but while Gurganus digs into the pasts that formed the sex maps of his pair, Baker leaves his likable man and woman relatively anonymous under the clothes they describe so well as they remove them. Yes, it's more like real life, and *Vox* is full of nice sexual quirks, like that sensuous elephant, yet one finishes the novel feeling it's all been a brilliant fuss about surface.

I'll continue to read Baker, and O'Brien too, despite my frustrations. But there are writers whom I have given up on completely. I feel that I never need to look at another book by Don DeLillo or Philip Roth. I almost included John Updike, except I once gave him up only to be won back before he lost me again. But the celebrated *Rabbit* tetralogy is Updike at his weakest: gorgeously described ugly environments serve as a stage for emotions that rarely rise above sour irritation. Updike's best work remains his early Olinger stories and novels, and later comic surprises like *Bech: A Book* and *The Coup*.

Jonathan Franzen's long, rambling essay in *Harper's*, "Perchance to Dream," on the declining cultural importance of the novel (he blames the age, but goes on to ask some interesting questions about what kind of people actually read serious fiction) intrigued me enough to pick up his second novel, *Strong Motion*. It's as ambitious as he said a novel should be—all about earthquake science and mass psychology—but dramatically loose and emotionally thin, resembling work by writers I think of as sons of Thomas Pynchon: William K. Vollman and David Foster Wallace. I'll give Franzen another chance—like Richard Powers, another Pynchoner from the DeLillo side of the family, he has more soul and craft than his sibs—but all these men treat story as little more than information processing, their primary goal seeming to be how much data they can download from chapter to chapter.

Note that my difficulty is with straight men, not straight white men. Race makes only so much difference. I like Ernest J. Gaines's lean, heartfelt novels, but he belongs to an older tradition of artful artlessness. John Edgar Wideman's memoir, *Brothers and Keepers*, is strong and startling, but his novels are as rhetorically busy and dramatically tired as those of his white counterparts.

What's going on here? Are the books at fault, or am I? As I said, reading is a highly subjective act, and I may be reading the wrong books or with the wrong sensibility. But I think my dissatisfaction with straight male fiction goes deeper.

So much of what these men write feels like old news to me, both in voice and content. There are too many good sons aping famous fathers. In addition to the sons of Pynchon are sons of Hemingway, like O'Brien and Robert Stone, and sons of Faulkner, like McCarthy (who copy the bad poetry but not what's great about Faulkner, his uncanny sense of structure and ability to create characters across class and race). Jay McInerney recently dropped Salinger for Fitzgerald. Ford switches fathers from book to book: his first novel, *A Piece of My Heart*, is Faulkner; his third, *The Sportswriter*, is Walker Percy; *Rock Springs*, his short story collection, is Raymond Carver with scenery. There are only a few Joyceans left, meta-language omnivores like Robert Coover and William Gass, but many Nabokovians, a richer vein where writers often capture the beauty and wit of the master without always getting his pity: Baker, Updike, Steven Millhauser, and even a gay man, Edmund White. (No, sexuality does not guarantee success either. Different as they are at their best, Updike and White sound surprisingly alike when they're off, filling the cracks with similar poetic tinsel.)

There's nothing wrong about beginning with borrowed bottles—most writing begins in a love of other writers—so long as you fill them with new wine. But there's too much old wine, much of which has gone flat or turned to vinegar. What was exciting in 1964 about *Herzog* by Saul Bellow was the novelty of an injured man dropping the stoic act and being hysterical. That Bellow's women were all luscious helpmates or castrating bitches was troubling yet in accord with his protagonist's fury. Well, straight men have been doing lonely Moses Herzog ever since—Ford as Frank Bascombe, Updike as Rabbit, Roth as Portnoy, Roth as Zuckerman, even Roth as Roth—using various masks to hide self-pity, secretly playing victim with the very relish that women and gay men are unjustly accused of indulging in their work.

Or they play know-it-all puppet master, like those sons of Pynchon. Authors can put themselves outside as well as inside their novels, but, either way, at least one other character must have some emotional or intellectual life if a book is to breathe. The flat figures sketched by an ice king of anxiety like DeLillo or a class clown like T. Coraghessan Boyle (*World's End, The Road to Wellville*) exist simply as chess pieces to be moved about by their creator. Nobody is as real, or right, or has half as much presence, as the all-knowing, game-playing novelist.

That is my chief problem with most straight male fiction: authorial egos are so insistently, domineeringly present. In too many novels I feel locked in a jail cell with just one other person, either a solitary sufferer or all-knowing puppeteer. Other people, other points of view, barely exist—even other male points of view. Without other voices, there's no drama, no doubt, no discovery. There is only the author, and if you've read one of his novels, you've read them all. DeLillo can offer nothing new each time out the gate except his latest metaphor for the awfulness of contemporary life. One can watch Philip Roth pursue another novel-writing alter ego, like a dog chasing its tail in front of a mirror, only so many times before the eyes glaze over, the mind goes numb.

The most visible symptom of this incurious egotism is the difficulty these authors have in creating believable women. Even Tim O'Brien, who writes about men in Vietnam with clear, cold empathy, draws a blank when he comes to the wife in *In the Lake of the Woods,* unable to imagine any role for her except to be unfaithful to her husband, or killed by him. When straight males want to get critical about masculinity, their men murder women. The bloodless little murders and compromises of everyday life, the bad deeds that any reader can see him- or herself committing, are too messy to bother with.

Which brings me to my other problem with these writers, their discomfort with the smaller, domestic emotions, the sweet even more than the bitter. They dread seeming at all sentimental. I suspect many men draw so heavily on the strategies of their elders out of a nervous need to give their work the cold stamp of art, any anxiety of influence offset by their fear of middlebrow sentimentality, the "feminine," if you will. But sentimentality is often just the name we give to a set of embarrassing yet real emotions, and a fear of sentiment too easily becomes a denial of any kind of feeling, except buried self-pity.

As a result, the male characters in these writers' works often come off as badly as the female. If you want to read about the loving if sometimes wrongheaded husbands and fathers of everyday life, you're more likely to find them in a novel by a woman than one by a man. *The Other Side* by Mary Gordon looks at first like that most middlebrow of genres, the family saga shaped around a dying grandparent. But this is a deep, artful book, written in compact, often lyric prose, full of history, real jobs, and merciless attention to emotional detail, an intimate epic of Irish-American life. Gordon crowds a working-class home in Queens with sharply rendered people: women pickled in spite, sadly stolid men, manic teenagers and two lawyer cousins, male and female, who strive to sustain heart and soul in the cozy wreckage. But Gordon's most striking twist is that the old husband, Vincent, is a warmer, gentler, more likable figure than his dying wife, Ellen:

> Ellen MacNamara made a happy marriage. But it was not enough. She came into it from a life already scalded by shame, stiffened by disappointment, judgment, fear. So her happy marriage could not make her a happy woman. Her husband's happy marriage almost made him a happy man.

Vincent, who has a temper, a fondness for sentimental music and a soothing love of machinery, is that most difficult thing to achieve in fiction, a plausible good man. Gordon explores Ellen's past and wounds, putting us inside the anger that Vincent has lived with all these years, showing us the cost of his love. The softer emotions do not produce ease and comfort, but make one vulnerable to whole new ranges of pain and responsibility.

A novelist myself, being gay does not protect me against failure. I don't always know how my books read, if the emotions I feel when I write, big and small, actually come through in print. But I do try. What depresses me about so much straight male fiction is that there's no indication of the author even wanting to dig into the homely confusions of tenderness, doubt, and guilt.

I should add that there are women and gay men whose books fail in egotistically masculine ways. Gore Vidal's imperial certainty, delightful in his essays, leaves his novels flat and lifeless; he knows what it all means before he puts a word on the page. Joan Didion's dry nerves cover her brittle novels like stylish cobwebs. Mona Simpson becomes so beguiled with her clear, snappy prose that she doesn't notice the point, usually halfway through each book, when she stops giving us anything fresh we can respond to. She resembles male chatterboxes like Mark Helprin, Norman Rush, and John Irving, virtuoso storytellers who sometimes engage real emotion and ideas but too often run on without direction or dramatic purpose.

Perhaps I've just read too much and approach new novels with excessively high expectations. But I don't really believe that my disappointments are simply those of a jaded reader—or of an envious writer studying the competition.

Recently, a friend taught an ethics class at a prominent business school, using novels and short stories as her texts. She inherited the course from a famous teacher whose reading list was full of the usual suspects: Fitzgerald, Bellow, Cheever, Miller. Anna was uncomfortable that it was all straight white men and wanted to add other voices. She did it tentatively at first, afraid she was being merely political. But she soon found that the new work—*Linden Hills* by Gloria Naylor, "Blessed Assurance" by Gurganus (another story from *White People*)—elicited a stronger, livelier response from students than the canonical books did. The old material more or less told the same story: the American dream can be a nightmare, which may have been news twenty years ago but isn't anymore, not even to future corporate executives. The new work, however, offered no simple message. "Blessed Assurance," for example, where a white businessman looks back on an awful, exploitative job in his youth when he sold funeral insurance to black people, only asked questions, difficult questions: How are we to act in an unjust world? Can good intentions produce good results? How do we live with ourselves when they don't?

Here recently, dredging all this up, I've decided: if a person's emotional life were only rational—if it just "came out" like algebra does—then none of us would ever need good listeners or psychiatrists, would we? We'd do nicely with our accountants. We'd bring our man a whole year of receipts, evidence and pain. We'd spend two hours together in a nice office and, at the end, our hired guy could just poke the

Tally button and we, his client, would feel clean again and solid, solvent. Nice work if you can get it.

Anna became bolder her second year, adding South African Nadine Gordimer, Indian-American Bharati Mukherjee, even a new straight man, Russell Banks, to her syllabus. I suggested some of these books. I was pleased to hear that work that moved me could set off sparks in others. The new books raised more questions. These authors hadn't come up with answers either, but wrestled honestly with mixed feelings and uncertain acts, providing a place where Anna's students could engage personal doubts and conflicts too messy to be addressed directly.

Perhaps this is the most valuable service that literary fiction can offer to readers. Other people's stories enable us to step out of cramped selves while remaining emotionally connected to our experience—human reality is nothing if not emotional—and take in more of life, including the half-rightness/half-wrongness of ourselves and others. This does not make good fiction a civics lesson full of moral uplift. The truth can be shockingly amoral. But I approach new novels with high hopes and special demands: tell me something I didn't know. Make me feel something I haven't felt, or forgot I could feel. Use emotion to put me inside somebody else's skin and complicate and confuse old certainties. Successful fiction seems to require not only emotion, but doubt, a skepticism that is partly emotional itself, built out of mixed feelings and confused sympathies.

I'm not sure why women and gay men seem to do this better right now than their straight male counterparts. Perhaps, as a fellow gay writer suggests, we've simply had more practice living in a gray zone where we feel a need to justify ourselves to others almost every hour of every day. Straight men now find that they too need to justify and explain themselves, and it angers them, causing them to shut out the world and turn up the volume of self. There is a siege mentality among straight male novelists. Out of fear of uncertainty and unease with mixed emotions, they take refuge in established models of greatness, technical virtuosity, and isolated egos.

It's odd that nobody has commented on this hardening of literary arteries. But then I might not have noticed it myself, would've blamed my indifference to their books on my own narrow gay point of view, if I hadn't stumbled upon straight male writers who could still move and excite me.

Because they *can* cross over, although it's not easy. Russell Banks in *The Sweet Hereafter* uses the voices of an old female bus driver, an angry New York lawyer, and an abused teenage girl, with such conviction that it seems effortless, like Tolstoy's ability to get into the heads of men, women, and horses. I shouldn't have been surprised to read Banks's essay in *The Movie That Changed My Life* on the bad effects of Walt Disney's *Bambi* and discover that Banks can be as scrupulously, self-mockingly PC as my more political gay or feminist friends. Enormous work went into the sympathetic curiosity that feels like second nature in his fiction.

Many straight men openly envy the audiences of "minority" writers, feeling their own tribe is too busy with Tom Clancy to read anything serious while we have our guaranteed little provinces—as if fiction were a matter of like writing to like. The truth is that the best female and gay writers tell stories that should engage anyone. No life, when written about honestly and clearly, is so alien that a good reader can't glimpse some common experience made new through a different lens. And these writers are not just writing up their identities but using their difference to see into the differences of others.

The women often get inside the otherness of masculine skins, as Smiley and Gordon do. Paul Russell, a gay novelist, treats the very straight, very difficult astronaut father in his heady, polyphonic novel *Sea of Tranquillity*, as an empathetic equal. The man goes to the moon and back—Russell puts a new spin on the phrase "distant father"—only to find himself soul-sick and stranded on earth. Too late, he works to reconnect with the wife and gay son he lost on his journey.

Carol Anshaw in *Aquamarine* does not just contrast straight and gay identities, but collapses them together. She opens with a teenage girl's sexual encounter at the Olympics, then imagines three alternate futures for the girl, three short novels where Jesse is a married woman in Missouri, a lesbian in New York, and a solitary divorcée in Florida. What stays the same from one life to the next is as revealing as what changes.

And in Mukherjee's *Jasmine*, the white characters are as deeply mixed and complex as the Indian ones. Mukherjee works against the dangerous myth that Third World people are somehow more real than others. Her twenty-four-year-old narrator has lived an overload of lives, from a childhood in a Punjab village to a home with a banker in Iowa, along the way seeing her husband killed in India and committing a murder herself.

She is confused and moved when privileged New Yorkers treat her as an equal.

> Even though I was just an *au pair,* professors would ask if I could help them with Sanskrit or Arabic, Devanagari or Gurumukhi script. I can read Urdu, not Arabic. I can't read Sanskrit. They had things they wanted me to translate, paintings they wanted me to decipher. They were very democratic that way. For them, experience leads to knowledge, or else it is wasted. For me, experience must be forgotten, or else it will kill.

Privilege here is treated not as corrupt but enviable, fortunate, an enabler of kindness that in turn leads to new risks. If suffering were good for you, we should want everyone to suffer. Mukherjee challenges our usual ranking of innocence and experience, which is just one of several themes in this rich, miraculously concentrated novel. I cannot guess which works here will become classics, but *Jasmine* is a powerful book that deserves to be read fifty years from now.

The flip side of straight male anemia is the weird invisibility of what I sincerely believe is an age of great American fiction. Many of the recent books I love were praised by reviewers, widely bought and read. Yet when critics do their overviews of American letters, editors make their end-of-the-year lists and juries award their prizes, these books somehow don't count. Is it still assumed that only art produced by a straight white male has any chance of being "universal"? Are we back in grade school where girls will read stories about anyone, but boys won't even pick up a book unless its protagonist is male?

We no longer hear about the Great American Novel, the old myth that a writer could somehow produce one book that would encompass everything important about the age in which we live. Modern life has become too vast, various, and articulate for such a beast. Over the past ten or fifteen years, however, we've seen the rise of Great American Fiction, not a single novel but a crowd of querulous, troubling, rigorously tender books that cumulatively capture the sorrow and health of contemporary life.

A few of these books are written by straight men. It's a pity that there aren't more. But until others climb down from the solitary statues of old masters, until more men crawl out of their cells and foxholes and recognize they are not alone in the world, there is a wealth of stories to move and sustain the rest of us.

Postscript, 1998

I wrote this essay a year and a half ago and was unable to find a home for it until now. I won't go into all my rejections, polite or brusque, from magazine editors, but want to discuss here a few developments during this time.

One of the novels I described, Nicholson Baker's *Vox*, briefly made the evening news when it appeared on the list of gifts from President Clinton to Monica Lewinsky. Commentators treated the book as soft porn, but I was impressed by the president's taste and sense of humor.

More relevant to this essay, however, was the publication of major new work from several writers I grumbled about: *Mason & Dixon* by Thomas Pynchon, *Underworld* by Don DeLillo, and *American Pastoral* by Philip Roth—1997 might be called the Year of the Testosterone Dinosaurs. I was never tempted to wade into Pynchon's eighteenth-century pastiche, yet decided to give DeLillo and Roth another chance. DeLillo's prose remains sharp and dry, like elegant patterns of pebbles, but his deadpan monotone and unyielding make-it-strange aesthetic reduce *Underworld* to an epic of affectlessness, an endless tale told by one of the autistic savants from Oliver Sacks's *An Anthropologist on Mars*. There are no people in this mammoth Martian tome, only data vectors with human names; I gave up after two hundred pages.

American Pastoral is more engaging and Roth actually wrote about someone other than himself this time, The Swede, a Jewish jock who achieves the American dream but loses it when his teenaged daughter becomes a terrorist. The narrator, however, is Roth's old alter ego, Nathan Zuckerman, and we're not allowed to forget that he is only imagining this story. The novel reads like an unedited first draft, full of hasty improvisation, abrupt backtracking and long patches of Jamesian woolgathering. And Zuckerman—or is it Roth?—does not have a clue on what it's like to be a good businessman or father. The daughter, Merry, is unconvincing and grotesque. There are enough strong passages and even scenes to keep one reading, but this is an exasperating novel, sluggish and false, with a garrulous third act so full of loose ends that the entire book topples down a black hole.

These behemoths by Pynchon, DeLillo, and Roth received

an uncommon amount of media attention, enough, one would think, to jump-start interest in literary fiction again. Instead, publishers reported a decline in sales. Sales were down in all categories, but I can't help thinking that many readers actually picked up one of these baggy monsters, bogged down in it and decided they'd been right to avoid serious novels. (My most electric male readings of the past two years were *A Fine Balance* by Rohinton Mistry, an Indian novelist; *Jack Maggs* by Peter Carey, who's Australian; two novels by gay Americans, *Plays Well With Others* by Allan Gurganus and *An Arrow's Flight* by Mark Merlis; and the novels and stories of Charles Baxter, a straight male recommended to me after I wrote my original essay, another exception as wide in his sympathies as Russell Banks; Baxter's novel *First Light* is especially good. Banks himself just published an ambitious historical novel, *Cloudsplitter*, about John Brown, which didn't get half the attention that the books by Roth and company did. I've not read it yet, but look forward to the experience, as I look forward to reading Richard Russo's last book, a comedy with the intriguing title *Straight Man*.)

Contradicting the decline in sales, however, and proving there is an audience for serious fiction out there, was the surprising success of Oprah's Book Club. Oprah Winfrey's choices are sometimes dismissed as "middlebrow," but none are trash, all are serious, and there is work by such strong talents as Toni Morrison, Kaye Gibbons, and Jane Smiley. I wish the Book Club would include more men, and an occasional gay or lesbian novel would be nice, but Winfrey has proved the existence of a hungry readership, people who need only to be told which good books might actually engage and speak to them.

So I am not without hope. The problem is not with writers or even readers (although I wish there were more of them), but with the book media, the magazine editors, regular reviewers, and list-makers who decide what's important. One could write a whole essay on the reputation machine, what it is, who's in it, why it does such a lousy job of matching books with readers. My guess is that it's dominated by men and women who have not really read fiction since college, twenty-plus years ago at the twilight of the Golden Age of Heterosexual Man. In the confusion of riches, they take refuge in the brand names and attitudes of the past. If only they could find the time to read for pleasure again, and discover some of the authors the rest of us are reading, we might see the spread of a literary culture as various and lively as the books themselves.

1999

A QUEER MONSTER:
HENRY JAMES AND THE
SEX QUESTION

—ᨇᨇ—

I am that queer monster, the artist.

—letter to HENRY ADAMS

1

ALMOST EVERYONE WHO has spent any
time with Henry James—his family,
friends, readers, even his critics and biographers—sooner or later becomes exasperated
with the man. He can be so articulately circumspect, aloof, and elusive, swaddling himself and his art in thickets of finely split hairs.
There's a frequent note of humbug to the
Master. You can't help wanting to kick him
now and then.

I often feel it myself, especially when reading the later fiction. If my mood isn't right, his beautiful garrulity—the manner enlarging on the matter—can sound just like W. C. Fields. The elaborate courtesies of his letters are often as maddening, his delicate ways of refusing to give a favor, his overly genteel methods of correction or criticism. The Master was a master of the passive/aggressive.

Yet I continue to read James, and books about James. I am not a true Jamesian—there are whole stretches of his work I cannot get through. I am able to read late James, "the Old Pretender," only when I'm in a certain, peculiar, vegetative state of mind. I explore him in isolated bursts, but he is a country that I visit regularly.

And he's a remarkable country, richer and more various than is often acknowledged. In *Washington Square*, *The Portrait of a Lady*, *The Ambassadors*, and other work considered essential James, he created complex parables of innocence and experience, dramatic accounts of the moral trade-offs required to gain pleasure, happiness, knowledge. Yet he also wrote *The Bostonians*, with its lively realism, high comedy, and moral unpredictability, a book that I believe is one of the great nineteenth-century American novels, right up there with *Moby Dick*, *Uncle Tom's Cabin*, and *The Adventures of Huckleberry Finn*. His life is fascinating, too, strange and mysterious and extraordinarily productive: eighteen novels (twenty if we count the plays, *The Other House* and *The Outcry*, that he didn't so much rewrite as simply reformat into fiction), over a hundred novellas, short stories and tales, scores of essays and reviews, several travel books, a biography, three volumes of autobiography, and a clutch of unsuccessful plays. He did it over a remarkably long career, publishing his first story in 1864 when he was twenty-one, and his last book, a collection of essays, in 1914, a year and a half before his death.

One special source of fascination—and another source of exasperation—is his sexuality. Whom did he love? Did he ever act on this love? How did it affect what he wrote? Should it affect how we read him?

The rise of gay studies and queer theory has put his sexuality front and center, much to the irritation of more traditional Jamesians. But there is a long history of speculation on the sex life of the Master. After all, this was a man who wrote constantly about love, yet never married and left no record of a consummated affair with *anyone.*

As far back as the 1920s, when talk about sex became more open, attention went to what James in a volume of autobiography, *Notes of a Son and Brother*, called "an obscure hurt," the injury he suffered as a young man while putting out a fire in the early days of the Civil War. It had something to do with a fence rail. (The autobiography is late James at his most circumspect). The rumor went out that he'd been castrated. Hemingway makes a joke about it in *The Sun Also Rises*. R. P. Blackmur alludes to it in a literary encyclopedia essay, comparing him to Abelard, that medieval castrato of the Holy Spirit.

Not until 1953, when Leon Edel published *Henry James: The Untried Years*, the first of his five volumes of biography, was it made clear that the "obscure hurt" was a back injury. More recent scholars have questioned even that, wondering if the injury were fictional or psychosomatic, an excuse for young

Henry's avoidance of military service in the Civil War. Illness and hypochondria ran deep in the James family. Their letters are full of talk of back trouble, nervous exhaustion, and (a favorite topic) constipation. Health issues often seem like the family substitute for sex.

The back injury, however, appeared to stop all discussion of James's love life, until 1969 and 1972 when Edel published his last two volumes, *Henry James: The Treacherous Years* and *Henry James: The Master*. And there it was in print, from a reputable scholar, solid accounts of the old man's infatuations with young men. The chief love was Hendrik Andersen, a Norwegian-American sculptor who met James in 1899. But there was also Morton Fullerton, Jocelyn Persse, Gaillard Lapsley, and Hugh Walpole. Like many readers of James, I often grumble about Edel, his doggedly Freudian readings, his tendency to lose the forest for the trees, his uncritical, possessive love (my Master right or wrong), but there is no denying the invaluable change he brought to our picture of James. He admitted that James's feelings for these men were romantic, erotic, although it appeared James never acted on his infatuations: Edel included the story that Hugh Walpole told a friend long after James's death, how he once offered himself to James only to have the old man clutch his capacious head in both hands and murmur, "I can't. I can't."

Very slowly, over the next twenty-five years, these revelations affected Jamesian scholarship. Combining with feminist and gay studies, they offered new ways of reading the man and his books. Yet the very thought of calling James homosexual still irritates people. Witness the storm of harrumphs over Sheldon Novick's 1996 biography, *Henry James: The Young Master*. Look at the way Lyndall Gordon dismisses all discussion of homosexuality in her otherwise fine book about James's friendships with women, *A Private Life of Henry James*. Even Philip Horne, in the introduction to his new collection of letters, *Henry James: A Life in Letters*, feels obligated to state that none of the letters he's seen resolves the sexuality question. (His selection, however, leaves out almost all letters that even *raise* the question, including those to Andersen and Fullerton.)

The first great James revival of the 1930s and 1940s took place in the shadow of the Popular Front and the Cold War. Many critics—Blackmur, Lionel Trilling, F. O. Matthiessen— were drawn to the man as an escape from ideology. "A sensibility so fine that no idea could violate it," T. S. Eliot famously wrote. The current James debates take place in an age of feminism and gay politics, and battles are being fought over his heart and genitals.

2

IN AUGUST 1904, Henry James, sixty-one, returned to America for the first time in twenty years. He'd been living in England, alone, a bachelor of the pen whose chief worldly pleasures were dining out and visiting the Continent. He had just completed his remarkable triumvirate of late novels, written (or rather, dictated) over four years: *The Ambassadors, The Wings of the Dove*, and *The Golden Bowl*. He shaved his beard in 1900—he had begun to look like the notorious politician

Boss Tweed—and now bore the huge, smooth, balding head of Humpty Dumpty, elegantly perched in the eggcup of a winged collar.

He arrived in New York, visited his friend Edith Wharton, then went up to Boston and Cambridge, the scene of his youth, where he stayed with his brother William and his family. He headed south, traveling alone and lecturing on "The Lesson of Balzac." He worked his way down the coast: Philadelphia, Richmond, and Charleston. He next took a train out west, where he'd never been, crossing the Great Plains and Rocky Mountains. Finally he came to a halt on the Pacific, at the Hotel del Coronado in Coronado Beach near San Diego, a white gingerbread monstrosity that would be used fifty years later by Billy Wilder as a 1920s Florida resort for the movie *Some Like It Hot.*

The emotions of the past months appear to have suddenly caught up with him at Coronado Beach. On March 29, 1905, he opened his travel notebook and began to fill the pages with words, impressions, memories.

A strange set of pages, they take up nearly two-thirds of the little brown book. There's nothing else quite like them in the published *The Notebooks of Henry James,* which are almost always about future writing projects without a trace of personal confession. Here James writes in a headlong stream of consciousness.

He begins with memories of Boston from his youth, the family house at Ashburton Place, his boarding house in Cambridge across the river, with glimpses of literary celebrity (James Russell Lowell, a visit by Dickens). Then, out of nowhere, a new thought stops him, a sudden recognition: "The point for me (for fatal, for impossible expansion) is that I knew there, had there, in the ghostly old C. that I sit and write of here by the strange Pacific, on the other side of the continent, *l'initiation premiere* (the divine, the unique), there and in Ashburton Place." And he lets loose with a surprising rush of feeling:

> Ah, the "epoch-making" weeks of the spring of 1865!—from the 1st days of April or so on to the summer (partly spent at Newport etc, partly at North Conway)! Something—some fine, superfine, supersubtle mystic breath of that may come in perhaps in *The Three Cities* [the travel book that eventually became *The American Scene*] in relation to any reference to the remembered Boston of the "prime." Ah, that pathetic, heroic little personal prime of my own, which stretched over into the following summer at Swampscott—'66—that of the Seven Weeks War, and of unforgettable gropings and findings and sufferings and strivings and play of sensibility and of inward passion there. The hours, the moments, the days come back to me—on into the early autumn before the move to Cambridge and with the sense, still, after such a lifetime, of particular little thrills and throbs and daydreams there.

And just when we're wondering what—or who—the hell he is talking about, he lurches into a new memory:

> I can't help, either, just touching with my pen-point (here, here, only here) the recollection of that (probably August) day, when I went up to Boston from Swampscott and called in Charles Street for news of O.W.H.

This was Oliver Wendell Holmes, future Chief Justice of the Supreme Court. James "vibrated so with the wonder and romance and curiosity and dim weak tender (oh, tender!) envy of it"—envy of Holmes, who was off in Europe that month. This leads to thoughts about his own move to England ten years later, then back to memories of reading *Felix Holt* by George Eliot that summer. Then:

> Oh strange little intensities of history, of ineffaceability; oh delicate little odd links in the long chain, kept unbroken for the fingers of one's tenderest touch! Sanctities, pieties, treasures, abysses!

3

"Little odd links," indeed. It was Sheldon Novick in *Henry James: The Young Master* who brought these pages from *The Notebooks* to my attention. They are the linchpin of his claim that James was not the bookish, disembodied virgin of reputation, but had a love affair in 1865—with young Oliver Wendell Holmes.

Many critics were instantly scornful of the possibility, seizing on various gaps in Novick's argument to dismiss the idea. I dismissed it myself when I read the pertinent pages out of sequence, using the book's index. But then I read the book itself, from start to finish, chasing down quotes as I read. I went to *The Notebooks* expecting the context would prove that James was only talking about the first excitement of writing, not sex. But the dates don't match up (James had been writing for quite some time before April 1865), and it doesn't really sound like the thrill of imaginative discovery. The full passage is so erotic, secretive, and strange that I am now convinced that Novick is on to something.

Novick does not make his case as well as he could have. His picture of the friendship between the two young men—Holmes twenty-four, James twenty-two—is buried in his account of the day-to-day of James's life. Novick abruptly drops the sex shoe at the end of a chapter, quoting the passage from the *Notebooks* on *l'initiation première*. He asserts that James must have meant sex and speaks as if the only mystery were the identity of his partner. He proposes Oliver Wendell Holmes, then scuttles off into an account of Lincoln's assassination. He does not get back to Holmes and James until nine pages later, while the reader is left scratching his head. (Novick never mentions the sudden appearance of Holmes in the notebook entry, popping up like a return of the repressed.)

The tale is more convincing with its dramatic momentum intact. Holmes returned wounded from the Civil War in 1864—the war that both Henry and his older brother William avoided. Holmes was a tall, lean, cynical fellow with a moustache, fond of women, literature, and, at this period, drinking. He started classes at Harvard Law School. He met Henry through William, who remained good friends with Holmes throughout his life. During the spring of 1865, after William left for Brazil on an expedition with the naturalist, Louis Agassiz, the puppy author began to spend more time with the young veteran. Henry was quite pretty in his early twenties, before he hid his face in a manly beard. When Henry went up to North Conway, New Hampshire, that summer to visit his cousin Minny Temple, he invited—no, he begged—Holmes to join him. Holmes did, bringing a friend from law school, another ex-soldier, John Gray. The three young men formed a circle around Minny Temple.

Leon Edel also gives enormous attention to this summer holiday, treating it as a humiliation for James. Edel assumes he was in love with Temple and lost her to Holmes and Gray. James reimagined the episode one year later in his 1867 short story "Poor Richard," about the love quadrangle of a young woman, two army officers, and an ineffectual civilian. Playing through Edel's biography, especially the later 1982 one-volume abridgement where he could be more direct, is the old saw that men become gay because they're afraid of women and aren't manly enough to get girlfriends. Temple died a few years later and, in death, became the model for both Isabel Archer in *The Portrait of a Lady* and Milly Theale in *The Wings of the Dove.*

For Novick, however, the sexual electricity was not between James and Temple, but between James and Holmes. He is somewhat coy about their affair, including too many "mights" and "maybes," sometimes out of honesty but also to add suspense. He incorporates quotes and phrases from the notebooks (such as "inward passion") without always identifying the source. One problem with his book stems from his decision to present events from a limited third-person point of view, keeping his camera in tight close-up on the James of the moment. This gives the book the immediacy of James's own experience, but locks Novick into the period under discussion.

A more intrusive biographical voice would have enabled him to range back and forth in time and explain his case better. He puts enormous trust in his readers, never guessing that many would read the book in bad faith. (He also assumes the reader knows a lot about James. He mentions the Gallerie d'Apollon at the Louvre and alludes to James's "famous dream" without giving details, expecting us to be already familiar with the strange dream of art and power where phantoms pursue each other in a dark palace during a lightning storm.)

Longer quotes from the notebook would have helped as well. Novick includes the first half of the sentence, "Ah, the 'epoch-making' weeks of the spring of 1865!"—but not the second half: "from the 1st days of April or so on to the summer (partly spent at Newport etc, partly at North Conway)!" The full quote makes the summer of 1865 part of James's excitement and puts Holmes squarely in the scene.

But Novick shores up the notebook entry with two remarkable letters that James wrote to Holmes in 1865, inviting him to come to North Conway. The first, dated July 14, raises the question of whether or not they will have to share a bed. James promises they will find another bed but adds, "I pant for August 1." Then, in the second letter, dated July 24, James says, "Of course one room is better than two, etc. If you don't mind it, I don't, as the young lady said when the puppy dog licked her face." The rest is silence—we don't know if the two young men shared a room, much less a bed, or where John Gray slept. The summer appears, however, to have cured James of his interest in Holmes. But there is a letter two years later, in the summer of 1867 when James was back in New

Hampshire writing reviews and "Osborne's Revenge," a story where romantic male friendship is spoiled by a woman's love. James tried to get Holmes to visit him and Holmes refused. James replied, "The brevity of your note broke my heart."

So there appears to have been *something* between James and Holmes, at least on James's side. It clearly meant more to James than to Holmes, but first love is often a one-way street. I am not convinced that they had sex. Oh, it's possible, and might explain how Henry's friendship could turn to love after a year of knowing Holmes. And what do we mean by sex here? A fuck? A handjob? A drunken wrestle? A kiss? Novick doesn't say, and rightly, too; but I remember a time when a hand on a knee could strike my heart like lightning. That phrase "inward passion" evokes something mild, as does, "my pathetic heroic little personal prime."

But the evidence suggests that if it wasn't sex, it was sexual. Novick does not make too much of all the sexual metaphors, the "throb" and "groping" and "tender" that sound like masturbation to the modern ear. James sensualized so many things that it's hard to say when his sensuality is code or unconscious or innocent. The prefaces to the *New York Edition*, written shortly after the notebook entry, are full of similar language, although nothing so rhapsodic or prolonged. In his footnotes Novick cites a comic juxtaposition from James's 1915 autobiographical essay, "Mr. and Mrs. Fields," where a digression about the Holmes family includes a surprisingly erotic description of the Bunker Hill monument with its "beveled capstone." Novick says its meaning is "unmistakable" when he should have called it deliberate, a private joke. After all, as Novick points out, this was a man who'd just named a character Fanny Assingham. I looked up the Fields essay, and the sensuous monument is there, in the middle of a lengthy discussion of young Holmes. But alongside it is the breastlike dome of the State House. If James *were* making a private joke about Holmes's penis, he was also admitting that the penis preferred women. This is wildly speculative, and I don't think Novick takes it any more seriously than I do. But the mind is a strange place—a writer's mind stranger still. Back in college, when I first fell in love with men but had not yet gone to bed with one, I found the mere sight of farm silos very disturbing.

I am projecting my own experience here, but readers as well as biographers bring their lives to a life story, just as jurors bring their experience to a trial. The trick is not to be blinded by subjectivity, but to use it to flesh out the evidence. I don't know if Novick is gay, but his own experience of love and sex must have provided the woof of the tapestry that he weaves here.

Novick argues that this love affair opened up James as a writer, so it's not irrelevant. The man who wrote so often about love must have been in love himself. He also makes a good case that James used Holmes twenty years later in *The Bostonians* (1886), as a model for Basil Ransom, the tall, lean, cynical Southerner with a moustache, the war veteran who woos and wins Verena Tarrant from his lesbian cousin, Olive Chancellor.

The rest of the biography is relatively straightforward. Novick's only other speculative leap comes in his account of James's friendship with Pavel Zhukovsky. A Russian painter and aesthete who later became part of Richard Wagner's entourage, Zhukovsky met James in Paris in 1876. (James knew him by his French name, Paul Joukovksy.) James later told Edmund Gosse how he once pined under a window on a rainy night in his youth, straining for a glimpse of an "unapproachable face." Novick connects this story to James's courtship of Zhukovsky, admitting that it's a leap, but we already know Zhukovksy as the first of James's many gay friends. Edel insists that Zhukovksy's homosexuality ruined their friendship, while both Novick and Fred Kaplan (in his 1992 *Henry James: Imagination of Genius*) assume that James was in love with the man. Zhukovksy continues James's love life after Holmes, so there's not a long, unbroken latency before the documented loves of the later years. The relationship ended in 1879 when James visited Zhukovsky in Naples, where the Russian was part of the bachelor circle around the Wagners. Edel claims that James was shocked by the circle's homosexuality (their "fantastic immoralities and aesthetics," as James said in a letter of the time), but Novick argues that James was not so prudish and was put off by other things, including jealousy that Zhukovksy had so little time for him. James refused to meet Wagner, cut the visit short and went north to Florence, where he began work on *The Portrait of a Lady*. Novick offers Zhukovsky as a model for *Portrait*'s chilly, manipulative aesthete, Gilbert Osmond, with James himself in the role of Madame Merle, the observer/panderer/unrequited lover.

4

YES, THE SEXUAL evidence here is highly circumstantial, but it hangs together. We are not trying a man for murder, we are only attempting to understand the sources of his art. Whether or not James had sex isn't as nearly important to our picture as the recognition that he fell in love long before he met Hendrik Andersen. He wrote constantly about love. He drew the matter of his novels from other books and the pressure of the marketplace, of course, but, as Novick argues, he must've been in love himself, sometime. Otherwise these love stories would feel mechanical and secondhand. The love in James's fiction is always problematic, but it's still love.

Novick is not the first writer to go looking for a first beloved. Back in the late 1970s, after the last volume of Edel's biography appeared, the gay novelist and critic Richard Hall offered another candidate: Henry's own brother, William. And the brothers were close, even when they were apart, defining themselves through and against each other. Hall argued in two long articles in *The New Republic* followed by a couple of scholarly essays that William's infantilizing and feminizing of his baby brother—"*I* play with boys who curse and swear," he said, refusing to let Henry join him—produced a longing and hunger in the junior sib, an unrequited love that ended in heartbreak with William's 1878 marriage to Alice Howe Gibben. (Curiously, Hall, too, cites the Edmund Gosse pining-under-the-window story, but with Henry spying on William. He speculates that the encounter took place in Rome in 1874, when the brothers were touring Italy together, yet offers no plausible guess about what Henry hoped or feared to see.)

It's a neat, Freudian solution. Even Edel liked it. The family drama becomes even more important—as William himself said, Henry was the native of no country but the James family—and,

for a man of Edel's generation, incest is somehow more acceptable than nasty old sodomy. He incorporated Hall's theory in
his one-volume abridgement, writing a new chapter on how
William's marriage angered and wounded Henry. Yet Henry
remained in love, according to Edel, identifying so strongly
with his straight brother that it was years before he could fall
in love with another man.

Maybe this is just my own experience as a brother talking—
I don't know if either Edel or Hall had brothers—but when
I read the letters, I find no note of romantic love or longing,
only the amiable noise of two smart, competitive, intimately
irritable siblings. And the chief notes of irritation, what *might*
be read as unrequited love, are all on William's side, a friendly
(and sometimes not so friendly) mocking and teasing. After
all, for years William was in the weaker position. Henry found
his vocation as a writer long before William overcame his black
moods and made his own career in psychology and philosophy. As for Henry being devastated by the marriage, the only
evidence in Henry's letters is a mild joke about the brothers
being "divorced." Edel must turn to the novel that James wrote
at this time, *Confidence*, yet another triangle tale about two men
and a woman, to build any kind of case. (Their sister, Alice, suffered a mental breakdown after the wedding, and some have
argued that *she* was in love with William—he must have been
terribly lovable—but the more likely cause of the breakdown,
as Jean Strouse suggests in her 1980 biography, *Alice James*, was
that William's marriage terrified her with thoughts about her
own future as an invalid and old maid.)

The brotherly love scenario is even more speculative and airy than Novick's hypothesis about James and Holmes. Reading reviews of Novick, however, one would think that he had broken all the rules of good scholarship and written porno-biography. Millicent Bell in the *Times Literary Supplement* charges that he "surrenders to the novelistic urge and . . . abandons the biographer's fidelity to provable facts. As if other scholars, including Edel, haven't made raids upon areas of experience difficult to "prove." Bell goes on to say, "Perhaps the determination to find a love plot here has too distractingly obsessed James's modern biographers. So much else goes on in life." One can't help suspecting that she's really complaining about a particular kind of "love plot," especially when Novick's discussion of James's sexuality, including the effects of his relationships on his fiction, takes up 20 or so pages in a book of 433 pages, roughly the same percentage the subject gets in Edel's one-volume edition.

5

IT'S REMARKABLE THAT, this late in time, talk of James's homosexuality can still raise hackles. Nobody denies the late infatuations—the emotion in the letters is undeniable. Instead they deny that this vein was in James all along and that it had any effect on his writing. The "don't call James gay" school of critics can be quite genteel in their disapproval, downright Jamesian at times, softly insisting that sex doesn't matter here—only they've softly insisted for so long that it clearly does matter. How curious that even incest should be preferred over the hint of mint. The antagonism comes from homophobia, of course, but a very complex, slippery variety. It's as if the very concept, the words themselves—homosexual, gay, lesbian—make certain critics nutty.

Lyndall Gordon's *A Private Life of Henry James* is a case in point. This is actually a very fine, freshly imagined look at James, intelligent and fearless, except when it touches on you-know-what. Gordon paints a convincing portrait of a secretive, fussy man who could not fully love his female friends, Minny Temple and the writer Constance Fenimore Woolson, until they were safely dead—a sort of necrophilic heterosexual. This "figure in the carpet"—James's famous phrase was originally Woolson's—weaves neatly into homosexuality, of course, but Gordon insists that James was "a complex person" and "to label him would be reductive"—as if homosexuality is ever simple. She admits that he was attracted to young men late in life, but, "They evoked sighs and self-pity, not great works." Gordon took a similar approach in *Virginia Woolf: A Writer's Life* with Woolf's love of women, treating *Orlando* as minor and the "affair" with Vita Sackville-West (the quotation marks are Gordon's) as just a bit of overaged schoolgirl role-playing. She refuses to take same-sex attachments seriously. (Her dismissal of Novick, Kaplan, and all "closet" readings of James leans heavily on an essay by Philip Horne, "Henry James: The Master and the 'Queer Affair' of 'The Pupil.'" But I hunted down the essay and it does not demolish gay readings as Gordon claims; it only argues for better, more precise ones.)

The fear of the *G*-word is so strong that even progressive work can turn muddy. The new collection of letters, *Dearly Beloved Friends: Henry James's Letters to Younger Men*, edited by

Susan E. Gunter and Steven H. Jobe, is a useful compilation of the homoerotic correspondance. But not only do we get James playing his games—and these letters show James at his most exasperating—we get the editors playing games as well, filling the introduction with so many qualifiers that they become just as exasperating. To quote from just one paragraph: "This is not to say . . . Rather . . . will not resolve . . . On the other hand . . . Yet at the same time . . ." But that's nothing compared to the weirdness of John R. Bradley's preface to his collection, *Henry James and Homo-Erotic Desire*. The book includes smart essays by David Van Leer and Gregory Woods, as well as an introduction by Sheldon Novick, but, lest we get the wrong idea, Bradley opens the book with this curious statement:

> It should be made clear at the outset, however, that there is no intention to claim James as a "gay novelist," or to see his fiction as "gay fiction.". . . Novelists who are known to have been homosexual have not infrequently been portrayed, by gay and straight critics alike, as having dealt with the subject in an obsessive way . . . but I have never thought that to have been with case with, say, Marcel Proust or E. M. Forster, both of whom dealt with homosexuality and much else besides, and I do not think it to have been the case with Henry James either. Jane Austen, after all, was not obsessively heterosexual, and no critic, to my knowledge, has accused her of being so.

These are the nervous words of a gun-shy critic trying to cover his gay-friendly ass. Heaven forbid that a writer might be obsessively homosexual, or even obsessively heterosexual for that matter. (And Austen is a very odd choice, since she never married and, as Terry Castle argues in her playfully titled essay "Was Jane Austen Gay?" her great emotional bond in life seems to have been with her sister Cassandra.) I am a "gay novelist" myself, but I too regularly deal with "homosexuality and much else besides," so I am not unfamiliar with this kind of backhanded compliment. ("Why it's not a gay novel at all, but a real book.")

The underlying assumption here is that anything "gay" is inherently narrow, an identity fixated on nothing but sex and guilt, with no connection to the rest of life, no chance for universality. James scholars will use such odd locutions as "non-heterosexual" to avoid the G-word, or even draw upon gay social constructionism to argue that there was no such thing as a homosexual in the nineteenth century. The label is anachronistic, they say, and James would've been appalled by the contemporary gay world of bars and gyms and sex clubs. But nobody is claiming that James was a Victorian Chelsea boy. And even today many men who call themselves gay live outside the subculture. Homosexuality is a loose, various, sprawling thing. One of the stranger beliefs in this debate is that gay life is monolithic, when in fact there are shades of gray and varieties of sexuality that spill in all directions, not just into the bisexual or pansexual, but into asexuality. As I grow older and leave my own "heroic little personal prime" behind me, the sexuality of celibacy looks less alien and more real, not an absence but a different presence.

6

THE NINETEENTH CENTURY was full of artistic bachelors, and not all of them were homosexual. Edgar Degas never married, yet his love of women's bodies is fully expressed in his paintings of washer women and ballet dancers. Johannes Brahms was another bachelor of art, avoiding marriage after a close call with Clara Schumann, although we have records of his constant flirtation with the opposite sex and his reluctant visits to brothels. (One young prostitute described him as very kind; he treated her "like a daughter.") And then there was Lewis Carroll, who left a record of *his* love in photographs, whimsical letters, and stunning children's stories. The heterosexual bachelors could be just as strange as James, but scholars have fewer qualms about digging around in *their* libidos.

What is the line by Degas? "There is art and there is life, and a man has only one heart." The great love of James's life, of course, was his art, his writing. Nobody can deny that. He really was, as he told Henry Adams in a letter in 1914, "that queer monster, the artist"—even without the modern meaning of the adjective. You might claim that he fled life by burying himself in art, but life has a way of catching up, especially with artists whose art remains alive.

The best single biography of James right now, to my mind, is *Henry James: Imagination of Genius* by Fred Kaplan, not just because Kaplan is a fine storyteller with a generous understanding of mixed emotions, but because he builds his narrative on James's professional career. The book is especially good on the dollars and cents of the writing trade. Kaplan also recognizes how artists make little deals with life in order to get the peace they need for their work. The maneuvers that Edel treats as a product of James's fear of women are treated by Kaplan as his way of keeping life simple for the sake of his art—with the implication that this was only the conscious part of the story. The rest of the story, of course, was that he felt no sexual desire for women. Kaplan sketches the emotional life indirectly. He skips over the North Conway summer of love, but suggests James's homosexuality early on with a quote from a travel essay about a pretty street urchin in Venice. Not until the friendship with Zhukovsky does he confront his sex life. But despite Kaplan's indirection and tact, several critics, including Bell and Horne, have grumbled that his James is too gay.

Kaplan concentrates on the life, but occasionally reads the life into the work. He offers an excellent gay reading of "The Beast in the Jungle," written in 1903 after James met Hendrik Andersen, as an allegory of what James now understood about himself. His regret over missing out on homosexual love was transposed into John Marcher's regret over understanding too late the love of a woman, May Bartram. (It's more direct and clear than Eve Sedgwick's famous 1986 essay, "The Beast in the Closet," which treats the story as unconscious autobiography. Bartram's tomb at the end echoes Marcher's "closet," only his closet—if I read Sedgwick right—contains not homosexuality per se, but all self-knowledge, including, in a closet within the closet, his sexuality. I actually like Sedgwick, even when I disagree with her. I wish she'd write in plainer English, but her prose is no more difficult than that of Blackmur, say, or late James himself.)

The best gay readings of James I've come upon are almost all in Kaplan's vein, delicate explorations of the fiction as allegories of self. These critics recognize how a novelist translates private emotions into art—in much the same way a good actor uses his or her personal experience to build a part. Writers write out of their unconscious, even a writer as conscious as James, and do not always understand when an emotion is autobiographical. I speak as a writer myself here. Again and again, often after the fact, I will realize that a piece of story that I thought was imaginary actually expresses a firsthand reality. I believe that something like this accounts for the shift in sympathy in *The Bostonians*. Only halfway through the novel does James begin to "identify" with Olive Chancellor, the lesbian spinster who is mocked for much of the story. We can't know if he understood *why* he identified with her, but he nevertheless made her the tragic heroine and moral center of the book.

There's an excellent gay reading of *The Ambassadors* in *The Genteel Tradition and the Sacred Rage* by Robert Dawidoff: He finds several stories in the novel, including "a comedy of male liberation" where the erotic presence of two young men, Chad Newsome and Little Bilham, are "the secret heart" of Lambert Strether's awakening. *Henry James and Sexuality* by Hugh Stevens is full of smart readings. Stevens has a weakness for psychosexual architecture—he makes more of an "ample backstairs" in "The Jolly Corner" than it probably deserves— but his description of James's letter-writing as sexual flirtation, the ultimate safe sex, rings true, and he does a good job of unpacking the same-sex elements in the plots of *Roderick Hudson*, *The Bostonians*, and *The Princess Casamassima*.

There is homosexuality scattered throughout James's work, not just in the usual suspect, "The Pupil," but elsewhere, translated and transmogrified into more conventional experiences, yet with the old conventions remade into things strange, original, and startling. As we continue to break apart and put back together this Humpty Dumpty of letters, sexuality does not take simplify James but gives him a whole new dimension.

7

SO DID HE go to bed with Oliver Wendell Holmes? Or was he only in love with him? Or were they just friends? Are Novick and I reading too much in the tea leaves of James's prose? I wish there were a few more pieces of evidence, however circumstantial. (A letter from Holmes might be nice, something along the lines of "WJ's pesky brother continues to hang about—I know not why." In his correspondence with Harold Laski in the 1920s, Holmes says Henry James was not a gentleman, and "I will say no more on that subject." Holmes was a snob late in life, however, and he may have been referring only to the James family's Irish roots.) But the possibility of sexual love has been raised, and I think it's a strong possibility, one that makes more sense than thwarted incest or sexless purity.

For me, the drama of what happened in 1865 is not nearly as interesting as the drama of James remembering it forty years later. Desire had become tangled with other things: memories of Cambridge, books read, authors met, his old dream of living in Europe. Yet I like to think that he could accept and even enjoy his old infatuation with Holmes—from the perspective of a new century.

James seemed more relaxed about his sexuality late in life, opened up by his infatuation with Andersen, calmed by his friendship with such "non-heterosexual" men as Howard Sturgis (another American expatriate) and Sturgis's life long companion, William Haynes (known as The Babe). An enormous change had taken place. He was in his sixties; perhaps the urge had softened just enough for him to accept it. He acknowledged and purged his regrets over missing out on sexual love in "The Beast in the Jungle." In the following years, when he revised his novels for the *New York Edition,* he would expand Caspar Goodwood's kiss in *Portrait of a Lady* into something deep and electric.

Even in a private notebook he could discuss his love for a man only indirectly. The author of *The Aspern Papers* understood too well the posthumous life of journals and letters. James loved to read gossipy literary biographies, but soon began burning his own correspondance. (He even burned his copy of his sister's privately printed diary, despite the fact that there were three other copies in the world.) One suspects that the letters from Andersen, Fullerton, and others—especially Fullerton, who was frankly bisexual—were not as discreet as his.

Gay historians treat the close of the nineteenth century as the end of the era of romantic friendship, when doctors gave a name to same-sex attachments, and male love was no longer innocent. But at the very time that one would expect James to draw away from such affections, he plunged into them. And it was not just doctors who were talking. Oscar Wilde was convicted of gross indecency in 1895. James followed the trial with appalled fascination. He loathed Wilde, despised him for being so glib and public, but his enemy's tragedy did not frighten him off. James suffered his own crisis during this period, a loss of faith in his life and work. The writing was not going well, his fiction no longer commanded top dollar. Constance Woolson died in Venice in 1894, a suicide. The following year, on the eve of Wilde's fall, James experienced the humiliating failure of his play, *Guy Domville*. His imagination was suddenly fascinated with sex, somewhat morbidly at times. He wrote *The Turn of the Screw* now, and began to work on that weird, often absurd, sex-obsessed garden party novel, *The Sacred Fount*. Then, during a visit to Rome, he met Hendrik Andersen. He had reached a point in his life where, despite the example of Wilde, he must have thought, "Oh, the hell with it."

Andersen was blond, handsome, high-minded, and self-involved, a twenty-seven-year-old artist from Rhode Island who sublimated his own sexuality by sculpting cold, monumental nudes. He enjoyed the attentions of an older, celebrated writer. When he visited James at Lamb House back in England, James dreamed of setting up a studio for him there. The famous shaving of the beard took place in time for Andersen's second visit. But Andersen never lived with James. He moved back to America and love ran its course in letters, which seems appropriate for this man of ink.

By the time James visited his homeland, he had replaced Andersen with other, more casual loves. He looked forward to seeing Andersen again, but their schedules didn't match. They did not meet up until the very end of the trip. Nevertheless, one day at the Hotel del Coronado in 1905, in the intoxicating rush of visiting his past on paper, James remembered a similar bundle of feelings for another man from his youth, and *almost* called those feelings love.

2003

TATTLE
TALE

—⁓—

I T'S NOT OFTEN that a novelist gets to read a book written by one of his characters.

All right, David Brock is not fictional. And he is hardly original to me. But a few years ago, when the author of *The Real Anita Hill* outed himself after being attacked by Frank Rich, I was inspired to write *Gossip*, a novel about a young gay conservative journalist who was a bit *like* David Brock.

A novel has its own imaginative truth and facts can block the imagination. I read a few right-wingers, including Brock, but made a point of not learning too much about Brock himself. After finishing a first draft, I was startled to learn that Brock, like my man, was doing a biography of Hillary Clinton. I never guessed, however, that his book, *The Seduction of Hillary Rodham*, would defend her. Nor did I imagine that he would soon renounce his "tribe," first in *Esquire* and now in his memoir, *Blinded by the Right: The Conscience of an Ex-Conservative*. Truth *is* stranger than fiction. But David Brock is a very strange man.

He grew up in New Jersey and Texas, the adopted son of middle-class Catholics. He fell in love with politics early—he was tape recording Jimmy Carter's speeches off television at fourteen. Editing his high school paper, he made enemies with his editorials, and had an affair with a female journalism teacher. He attended Berkeley chiefly to spite his conservative father. He came out as a gay man there, but work on the university newspaper led him into Republican politics. His boyfriend moved with him to D.C. when he took a job at the *Washington Times*. Then, as he rose in far right circles, first at the Heritage Foundation and later the *American Spectator*, Brock drew away from gay life. There was an amicable breakup with his lover (who remains Brock's most loyal friend throughout this book). When his bestseller, *The Real Anita Hill*, made him rich and famous, he disappeared competely into the closet.

This is the classic tale of a man losing his soul before he regains it. Brock does not always tell the story well. He constantly chastises himself—"I was a whore for the cash," "I would go lower still," "my faculties were seriously impaired by . . . a sick sense of my own identity"—with a quickness that makes his behavior harder to understand. His confessions of old crimes—the distorted writing about Hill, the Clintons and others; his ratting on the friend of a friend to force the man to take a stand; his attempt to blackmail a woman into retracting a statement about Clarence Thomas—can sound like testimony at an AA meeting, sincerely meant yet disconnected, even robotic.

Brock accepts most of the blame, but often shares blame with peers. *The Real Anita Hill* had "four coauthors," he says, and names friends who gave him bad advice or dishonest information. His reluctance to write the notorious "Troopergate" article in the *Spectator* (which led to Paula Jones, which led to Monica Lewinsky) was overcome by warm words from one of his "surrogate parents," Judge Lawrence Silberman. The Silbermans, the judge, and his wife, Ricky, come in for some very bitter criticism. Other attacked associates include: R. Emmett Tyrell, publisher of the *Spectator*, who regularly dipped into business funds for personal use; Ted Olson, now advocate general at the Supreme Court, who denies being part of the well-funded anti-Clinton Arkansas Project; and Laura Ingraham, one of those pretty GOP attack blonds who appear on *Politically Incorrect*, a neo-homophobe who is shown here barhopping and snorting cat tranquilizers.

Brock puts himself in a difficult position. He's a tattletale. I resisted at first—he can seem petty and personal—even as I recognized that the Republican right was more petty and personal. If Hollywood is high school with money, Washington in the age of Gingrich was high school with CNN and subpoenas. There is no high road here and Brock is fighting fire with fire.

The autobiographical sections of the book are awkward yet convincing. The journalism portion, however, an inside history of the right, is first-rate, and not simply because Brock says the things I want to hear. *The Real Anita Hill* felt padded, its long-winded assertions built on a handful of "facts." Here Brock has tons of material. I don't know for certain if it's all facts or some "facts," but the sheer weight of matter gives his prose clarity and conviction. He supports or extends more conventional accounts of the era, such as *A Vast Conspiracy* by Jeffrey Toobin. He gets it all: the Bill-and-Hillary-hating millionaires, lawyer wolfpacks, and journalistic hacks. He shows the steady escalation of Clinton hatred from resentment to blind fury to insane delusion. Here was a moderate Democrat often indistinguishable from a moderate Republican, yet he was reviled as if he were Hitler or the Godfather. The Clinton-haters successfully suckered the so-called liberal media into sharing their madness. Historians twenty years from now will find this campaign as ugly and irrational as we now find the burning of witches.

Brock's conversion did not come like a vision on the road to Damascus. It built slowly. When *Strange Justice* by Jane Mayer and Jill Abramson, their account of the Thomas/Hill fight, was published in 1994, Ricky Silberman, a devout Thomas supporter, blurted over the phone, "He did it, didn't he?" Doubt set in, but Brock went ahead and attacked the book in the *Spectator*. He went ahead and took a million dollar advance from Simon and Schuster for his book on Hillary Clinton. The publisher assumed he would do to her what he did to Anita Hill. But his heart was no longer in it. As he investigated the thicket of charges around Whitewater, Vincent Foster, Travelgate, and the rest, he found no evidence of wrongdoing. He stopped believing his friends. He tried to write the truth.

The right-wingers who seemed to accept his homosexuality now damned him for defending Hillary. He was called a sellout. He was disinvited to parties. A straight friend later confided that these people had excoriated him all along in private for being gay.

He officially broke with his old friends one year later in an article in *Esquire*, "Confessions of a Right-Wing Hit Man." He even apologized to Anita Hill, first by letter, then in public.

I expected to dislike this book. I questioned Brock's motives. I suspected he was changing sides only from dissatisfaction, opportunism, or boredom. But I believe his book. He won me over, not through fine prose or clever wit or deep psychological analysis, but by a steady, graceless, honest rain of anecdotes and details.

When I wrote *Gossip*, I presumed my fictional gay Republican was more naive and less conscious than Brock. Friends were surprised by how sympathetic, if not entirely likable, I made my character. (Brock, by the way, never mentions my novel.) But the real David Brock is not only stranger than fiction, he is richer and more profound. He sounds slightly nutty at times, but I can't imagine anyone coming through such enormous changes without getting a little crazy. I am deeply impressed by his decision and ability to break with a world that loved him for the wrong reasons.

This is an amazing story.

2002

A SORT OF FRIENDSHIP:
A FEW THOUGHTS ABOUT GAY MARRIAGE

—∿—

M Y BOYFRIEND AND I have been together for twenty-five years. Neither of us is terribly excited by the idea of gay marriage. We have friends who love it and others who are appalled. Draper and I feel more casual about it. We don't want to get married ourselves (we met with a lawyer fifteen years ago and he set up the necessary wills and legal protections), but we're not going to stop you.

All right, *we* is a highly unstable word, and Draper and I are not one homogenized mind.

We agree more than we disagree, but I should focus on my own thoughts here. As our country goes marriage mad, I wonder why I am so nonchalant, curious yet detached. I'm going to explore a few ideas in an attempt to discover what I really think.

A sort of friendship recognized by the police.

—ROBERT LOUIS STEVENSON (on marriage)

UNTIL RECENTLY, LATE in the twentieth century, marriage was virtually mandatory for everyone. The West was as adamant about it as the Third World. A man without a wife was not a real man. A woman without a husband was a nonperson. That's no longer true in secular countries. More and more people live alone or in nonromantic households. More and more straight couples live together without the blessing of church or state.

Not only is marriage no longer required, there are fewer benefits to being married. Not enough companies offer decent health care to their employees anymore, much less to their employees' spouses. Most couples, straight as well as gay, include *two* workers, so individuals have their own Social Security accounts. And so on. (One exceptional benefit, however, is when your lover is a foreign national. Straight people can turn lovers into citizens simply by marrying them. We can't.)

Now that marriage is no longer a necessity, it's become more important as a symbol. And symbols are very interesting, not least because we are free to choose or reject them.

———

Love is not so much an emotion as a situation.

—LAURENCE STERNE

THE WORLD IS an unreal place. We want companions to provide a few landmarks to let us know where we are. Friends help
but a longterm mate is even better. Yet a mate can be just as
unreal, so we often require some kind of act or rite or magic
words to make the bond less ephemeral, less existential.

Progressive types who oppose any kind of marriage argue
that it brings the church and state into our bedrooms. Which
it does, but that's not how it feels. The experience of getting
married is more like a social ritual that pins down a slippery
emotion. Such as a funeral. I'm not being satirical. Love is as
powerful as grief; a wedding can shape and name love just
a funeral can shape and name loss. A wedding is a beautiful
thing, and much less conclusive than a funeral.

———

Two heads, four arms, four legs—
Such a delicate monster.

—THE TEMPEST

WHEN CALIBAN, A very rough monster, speaks these words
in Shakespeare's grand play about love and forgiveness, he's
referring to two men lying in a heap on the ground, but one
can't help thinking of a married couple.

Shakespeare is full of great marriage matter. There's "Let me not to the marriage of true minds / Admit impediments" from Sonnet 116, for example. His comedies often end in multiple weddings. The entire state of Massachusetts on May 17, 2004, when gay people were suddenly free to marry, resembled nothing so much as the finale of a Shakespeare comedy. My cousin Maureen got married to Meg, her lover of many years, that morning in a city hall on Cape Cod. Their stories about the festive day were absolutely exhilarating.

But the wonderful metaphor of marriage is also a legal fact, and legal facts involve lawyers.

I like lawyers. Some of my best friends practice law. My sister-in-law, whom, I adore, is a lawyer. However, I get very nervous whenever an enterprise requires an attorney. A few years ago a friend was involved in a small business contract that bound him to a financial partner he came to despise. It took them forever to dissolve the contract. And what is marriage but a very small, very personal business? More than one gay or lesbian attorney has quipped in recent years, "When gay marriage is legal, I'm getting out of legal aid into divorce law. That's where the money will be."

This spoils the metaphor for me.

It is not good for man to be alone.

—GENESIS, 2-18

ONE THING I love about gay marriage, without reservation, is how the very idea of it infuriates Christian conservatives. Liberal Christians respond more loosely and sanely, but conservatives—evangelicals, fundamentalists, Mormons, and so on—go bananas. That's because the concept strikes not just at their idea of gay people, but at their idea of themselves. The human race is full of sin, but conservatives have somehow decided that the gravest sin is homosexuality. Since they're not homosexual themselves, they can feel assured they are among the righteous, even if they sometimes think impure thoughts, cheat in business, cheat on their spouses, neglect their children or skip church on Sunday. Suddenly, gay people can marry too, and the good Christian must ask him or herself, "Is my life so different from theirs? Am I really so much better? Can I still count on heaven?" It has to hurt, to have your chief guarantee of eternal life snatched away, leaving you with the fear that you still might burn in hell after all.

*Marriage is a fine institution—but who wants
to live in an institution?*

—GROUCHO MARX

I MUST CONFESS that, as a novelist, I *love* gay marriage. Novelists tend to be descriptive rather than prescriptive in our morals. All we want is a good story. Where would the Victorian novel be without marriage? Where would postwar American fiction be without divorce? I can't wait to see what new plots and story lines gay marriage will provide.

However, I don't expect it to produce a radical change in perception or behavior. That's probably the chief reason for my laidback attitude. The change in perception has already occurred. Twenty years ago, gay marriage would've overturned American assumptions about gay people: oh wow, they love and live in couples, too. Now, however, many straight people, especially those who can look honestly at their own marriages, know gay couples are often like straight couples, no better and no worse.

People will behave much as they did before, only under different names. Some gay people will marry, others won't. Some marriages will work, some will go down in flames. Love is difficult with or without lawyers. A few years ago Andrew Sullivan argued that gay men needed marriage so we would learn to keep our dicks in our pants. Since then we have discovered that Andrew—with his love of chat rooms, sex lines, and testosterone injections—is the one with the wandering penis problem. However, I can't imagine a wedding ring will make him or anyone else more restrained than they already are. (A straight woman friend recently confessed that she found married men's wedding rings very hot—when they weren't married to her anyway. Some gay people are sure to find the band of gold even sexier than tattoos or pierced nipples.)

Marriage has loosened up in this country without disappearing. Now it's loose enough to include us. It's neither the end of civilization, as many Republicans claim, nor the guarantee of equal rights and domestic happiness that its giddier celebrants (often single) hope for. But gay marriage is going to happen, no matter what you or I or Jerry Falwell say. I wish the new couples all the happiness in the world, warn them they will have bad days as well as good days, and hope they understand that it never hurts to know a good attorney.

2004

AN EMBARRASSMENT
OF BOOKS

—⁓—

THERE SEEM TO be a lot of people
out there who can't wait to declare us
dead and buried. They say that gay people
don't need their own books anymore. We're
assimilated now. We have civil rights—well,
in some states and cities anyway. We have
Barney Frank. We have Gay Republicans. We
have *Will and Grace*. We don't need gay bookstores. We don't even need gay books.

Some of these naysayers are in places that
you'd expect, like the *New York Times*. Martin
Arnold, former publishing columnist there,

seized on St. Martin's decision to phase out their Stonewall Inn editions plus the recent near-closing of Oscar Wilde bookstore to declare gay books a thing of the past—they are so twentieth century. Other naysayers are more surprising. Last year *Out* magazine ran the new epilogue that Ed White wrote for *A Boy's Own Story* as if it were an epilogue for gay fiction. It was fun while it lasted, he said, but our days our numbered, especially now that "gay subject matter has been taken up by the more popular medium of sitcoms." Who would have guessed that a half-hour TV show would mark the end of civilization as we know it?

I'm a writer of gay fiction myself, so maybe I'm not the most objective judge here. But looking at things as a gay reader, the world looks very different.

Some years are better than others but there's almost always something new I can't wait to read. Last year we had Carol Anshaw and Adam Haslett and Neil Miller and Jamie O'Neill and Colm Toibin and— well, you heard the nominations and winners. It was a great year. This year we have, well, I have a new novel due out, *Lives of the Circus Animals*—I might as well plug that. But there's also a terrific new book by Mark Merlis, *Man about Town*, about a forty-something bureaucrat in Washington, D.C., and a powerful novel by Paul Russell, *War Against the Animals*, like *Middlemarch* with gay and straight people in a small town in upstate New York, and a beautiful first novel by Philip Gambone, *Beijing*, which immerses you in contemporary China the way that Isherwood's *Berlin Stories* immersed you in thirties Germany. There's a fine book of essays from Michael Klein, Michael Bronski's loopy anthology of pulp fiction, new books of poems from Henri Cole and Marilyn Hacker, Anne Carson's imaginative translations of Sappho, and—I'm talking only about the books I've read, sometimes in galleys or manuscript, so I'm talking only about writers I already know. But it promises to be a very good year.

Dead and buried, indeed.

The problem isn't that we don't have enough good books or writers, but that we need more good readers. Which is what groups like the Publishing Triangle have always been about, finding new people and introducing them to books, sort of like Date Bait for literature. But let's admit an ugly truth here: real readers—hungry, curious, open-minded readers of fiction in particular and good books in general—gay and straight—are a minority, every bit as freakish as the minorities that make up the alphabet soup of the LGBT. With gay readers or queer readers or lesbian-gay-bisexual-transgendered readers—whatever you want to call us—we're talking about a minority of a minority. (I've been using "gay" in the old-fashioned 1940s sense, when it meant men *and* women, and everyone in between, and anyone who was kind of funny. There's something funny about readers, too.)

A friend in D.C. has a new boyfriend who was startled to hear I write gay novels. "A gay novel? What's that? I don't have to read gay novels," he said. "I'm too busy living a gay life." I might add that this is a man who owns *eight* different biographies of Barbra Streisand.

But for many people, gay and straight, there are books and there is life, and books still feel like homework. Nowadays, as more of our novels are taught in college, I sometimes wonder if we lose part of our appeal. We're no longer forbidden fruit, so to speak. In the bookcases of thirty-somethings who keep the last books they read, meaning what they read in college, you sometimes see copies of *Dancer from the Dance* and *Bastard out of Carolina* next to *The Great Gatsby* and *Native Son,* incorporated into the decor like wallpaper. Which is not a bad place to be, although there are other places.

But we're not the only game in town anymore. Foreign film found a huge audience in this country during the fifties and sixties for the simple reason that it told dirty stories that Hollywood wasn't ready to touch. And we all want dirty stories, so badly that we'll even wade through high culture to get them. Once American movies were free to address such subjects as call girls and extramarital affairs and teenage boys having sex with warm apple pies, foreign film lost much of its allure—although it's interesting to note how many *gay* foreign films get released in this country. We still want stories about ourselves, so much that we'll even read subtitles.

People used to joke that the *Advocate* gave more attention to the movies that weren't being made than to the books that were being written. Now the movies are being made, some good, some bad, plus programs on cable TV, *and* that damned sitcom, and the *Advocate* still gives us two or three pages every issue. Thank God.

Because gay and lesbian readers are still out there. But they're a slippery, nebulous, fickle bunch. I read their reviews on Amazon.com, not just of my books but of friends and rivals.

I hear from reading groups in different parts of the country, and even meet with one here in New York, a large, friendly pack moderated by Joel Weinberg, Adam Kent, and others that gets together at the Community Center every month to discuss a new title. In fact, they're there tonight. I've met with them three times now, and they ask smart questions and make smart comments. They are not uncritical. But it's a joy, and a relief, to meet strangers who actually read your work and take something from it. I've sat in on their discussions of other writers, too, and they're highly opinionated, sometimes judging fictional people by much tougher standards than they judge the people they know, but fiction lets you do that.

And there are my own friends, many of whom are big readers: Geoffrey, Schuyler, Bryan, Michelle, and David, who are all here tonight. We pass books on to each other, recommend new titles, and warn each other off others. We don't always like or even read the same things. We're all Paul Russell fans; that's one thing we have in common. But only Geoffrey and I share Iris Murdoch; Schuyler and I do Henry David Thoreau and tales of the lying media, and the old Abercrombie and Fitch catalog; Bryan is heavily into science fiction, where I can't follow because I have a mental block about characters whose names seem to be all consonants; Michelle and I are both wild about Charles Baxter—and if you don't know Charles Baxter, you got to read *Feast of Love*; while David and I share Alan Hollinghurst and books on Pope Pius IX. No, they're not all gay books, and they're not all fiction either, but this is how real readers read.

This kind of activity writes white upon the culture page.

It's too scattered, too diverse. It passes under the radar of American social statistics. Readers are an ornery, unpredictable population. I mean, we don't only read *new* books. We sometimes read *old* books. We even read books by people who've been dead for a hundred years. It must drive publishers crazy.

And gay readers are a minority in a minority, the ten percent of the ten percent. When you stop to think about it, it's amazing how much influence we have had.

One thing I'd like to change, and I don't know how to do it, is to get more of that other minority, serious straight readers, to read gay books now and then. I want them to read us as easily as we read them. Because the best writers are saying things that can interest anyone. We saw it happen in theater with *Angels in America.* You see it now on cable TV with a great, nervy show like *Six Feet Under* and even a weird show like *Oz*—which seems aimed at gay men, and straight women with really kinky fantasy lives. So why not books? Are readers too genteel? Is a book too private and intimate, too literally in-your-face? Some people call *The Hours* a breakthrough, but *The Hours* was a stealth novel, and as Michael Cunningham said in an interview, "I can't help noticing that as soon as I write a novel without a blowjob, they give me the Pulitzer Prize."

Gay people who don't read gay fiction like to complain about it—it makes them feel better about not reading. The most common complaints are that it's not as good as straight fiction, which is nonsense, and that it's nothing but coming-out stories. I've been in this business exactly twenty-five years

now—I published my first short story in *Christopher Street* magazine in 1978, plucked from the slush pile by Patrick Merla,
who's also here tonight. But for twenty-five years, I've been
hearing, "There are too many coming-out novels, it's nothing but coming-out novels, when are we going to get past the
coming-out novel"—when, in fact, I have to sit down and think
really hard before I can name any book that qualifies as *just* a
coming-out novel. It's a little like complaining that Victorian
fiction is all marriage novels. Which it is, but marriage is only
the beginning.

Still, it's a revealing complaint. Because all gay people have
to come out, in one way or another. And it embarrasses us.
It's not quite gay self-hatred, but softer, more like gay self-
consciousness, gay embarrassment. We're embarrassed that we
have to come out. We're embarrassed that we have all these
stories to tell. We're embarrassed that there's all these books
we haven't read yet. We have an embarrassment of books, a
wonderful embarrassment.

Journalists don't read much fiction, even book journalists.
They're too busy studying maps to visit the places. Gay books
are no longer the new new thing; the only fresh observation to
make about them is that they're over, even when they're not.
But American culture—no, it's wider than that—the world at
large has never been entirely comfortable with books. People
would like to read them, they know they should, they sometimes enjoy them when they do. But they'd rather not. Except
for a few freaks, funny people like myself who read books the
way I used to smoke cigarettes. Funny people like most of you

here tonight, who are going to go home and read something before you go to sleep. But not two of you, I bet, are going to be reading the same book. All right, maybe two, but certainly not three.

Because we are such a strange, contradictory, grab-bag minority. We are all so different. We're a marketing nightmare and the ultimate model of diversity, and for that I say thank you.

Read at the Publishing Triangle Awards
on receiving the Bill Whitehead Award
May 8, 2003

IN MEMORY OF
OSCAR WILDE
(BOOKSTORE)

———

I AM A BOOKSTORE addict. I visit bookstores the way other people visit bars. I
worked in one for seven years, but even that
didn't cure me.

I first visited Oscar Wilde Bookstore in
1978, the summer after I moved to New
York. I was twenty-six but I was still coming
out. I went to my first gay bar that spring.
I attended my first gay party a month later
and went home with a grad student. I had
a better time than he did, but he suggested
we meet the following weekend at "that gay

bookstore in the Village." I was more excited about going to a new bookstore, a gay one no less, than I was about seeing this guy again.

The store was nothing special, just the front room of a small shop on Christopher Street. There were apartments upstairs. The basement level was used for storage. (Not until ten years later did Greenwich Village landlords begin to rent out basements for shops and homes.) The bookshelves were unpainted wood and half empty. Remember, this was 1978 and the new gay literature was just beginning to appear. I was disappointed there wasn't more, but I bought a book just the same. (I still remember which one: *The Church and the Homosexual* by John J. McNeill.)

Years passed. I met Draper and moved in with him a few blocks away. I returned to Oscar Wilde now and then and noticed the large, grumpy man in the office in back, Craig Rodwell. It was not a terribly inviting place. The stock was unpredictable: Rodwell often changed his mind about what could and couldn't be carried. When Different Light Bookstore opened on Hudson Street in 1983, I went there instead. I loved the wider variety of books and I thoroughly enjoyed the people. The staff was young, smart, and friendly. We regularly discussed literature, politics, movies, and music. I'm still good friends with several former clerks and managers. (Hello, Mark, Roz, Bunny, Ana, and Richard.) I got to know some customers, too, including a smart-mouthed mail lady named Kim Brinster who frequently visited the store in her butch post office uniform.

More time passed. Different Light moved uptown to a bigger space in Chelsea. One day in 1996 I visited Oscar Wilde again during one of my bookstore walks and found the place totally changed. The back office had been opened up; better shelves had been installed. It was very classy. There was a new manager, too: Kim Brinster. She had left the post office to work for a bookstore in Texas; the Texas store then bought Oscar Wilde and sent Kim up to manage it. Which she did for the next thirteen years. Owners changed—the man in Texas sold the store to a man in D.C. who sold it to Kim and her partner, Janet Layard-Liesching—but it was always Kim's store. She put her professional stamp on it, and her personality, a no-nonsense toughness that's also humorous, good-natured, and miraculously sane. She attracted a first-rate staff, too, as smart and eager as the kids at the old Different Light. The store was better than it had even been. I visited at least once a week.

But the book business was changing. Shortly after Different Light moved to Chelsea, a Barnes and Noble Superstore opened nearby. Then Amazon appeared, reinventing the book market for everyone. Independent bookstores began to close all over the country—the gay and lesbian stores actually held on longer than most.

The neighborhood was changing, too. The storefront that housed Different Light on Hudson Street became a maternity shop (called Belly Dance). Yet people continued to come to Oscar Wilde. It still attracted students who were just coming out. It was very popular with gay tourists, both American and European. Kim was tireless in finding new ways to sell books, whether online or at events around the city, especially the Lesbian and Gay Community Center.

Then, in October, the bottom dropped out of everything. First the Euro fell, which meant New York lost the foreigners who'd become a major part of Oscar Wilde's trade. A lean Christmas season followed, which hurt retail everywhere. The store needed the fat of Christmas to get through the winter, but there was no fat and things were not going to improve soon. The entire publishing industry was bleeding. So Kim decided to close the store.

Well-meaning folks in search of silver linings were heard to say that the closing was actually a good sign: gay people are fully accepted now and we don't need our own bookstore. It's an amazingly stupid statement in so many ways, but especially when all kinds of bookstores (all kinds of stores, for that matter) are failing.

I continued to visit during the last weeks while the stock was sold off and strangers dropped by to offer advice, like Job's comforters. It got a little grim. As Kim herself said, "It's like a long wake."

I am writing this two weeks before the store's final day, but I feel like I'm in mourning. Not for Kim—she has better opportunities ahead of her—and not even for the store. No, it's for a way of life I fear we are losing, bookstore life, an old-fashioned mix of shoptalk and community, literature and commerce. You don't get the same experience when you buy a book online and write comments at your computer. You don't get it when you enter a warehouse of a store and browse the shelves anonymously. Sometimes anonymity is good for readers—books are awfully intimate—yet it's good to come out of your solitude and make small talk over the printed page.

A bookstore like Oscar Wilde was a wonderful place for doing that—a place where thinking people could be alone *and* be together. I'm having a hard time imagining my life without it.

2009

PERRY STREET
REDUX

——ᵕᵕ——

I AM BACK ON our front stoop again, at the end of the first decade of a new millennium. I am reading—as usual. It's a lovely late afternoon in the spring and Draper is upstairs at his computer editing a friend's documentary. I am waiting for him to finish so we can go for a walk before dinner.

I'm reading *Exile's Return*, Malcolm Cowley's lively, impressionistic account of his generation of writers in the 1920s. Greenwich Village was a major site of their comings and goings. I recognize many of the streets he mentions.

Suddenly Cowley is describing the address directly next door. The brownstone on my left was the home of Squarcialupi's Restaurant in 1924. It was a spaghetti joint, located in the basement. Cowley, Hart Crane, Allen Tate, Caroline Gordon, and others used to come here to eat cheap pasta, drink red wine, read their poetry aloud, and play songs like "Too Much Mustard" on the piano.

"We were all about twenty-six, a good age, and looked no older; we were interested only in writing and keeping alive while we wrote, and we had the feeling of being invulnerable," writes Cowley. "We didn't see how anything in the world could ever touch us, certainly not the crazy desire to earn and spend more money and be pointed out as prominent people."

I sit up and take a deep breath, amazed. The building is now the home of Cynthia Rowley, owner of a chain of pricey dress shops. You can't get more prominent or earn and spend more money. She installed a swimming pool out back for her two daughters—we hear them splashing and screeching in the summer. There are more children in the neighborhood than there used to be, which has its charms as well as its annoyances. Back in the 1980s, the Rowley building had a crack den in the basement, its windows broken and stuffed with mattresses. I don't miss the mornings when I left for work and found blood splashed on the pavement like paint and a police car at the curb. But in eighty-odd years the address next door has gone from poets to crack addicts to Cynthia Rowley.

Our neighborhood has changed. Our building has changed as well. Our stoop isn't nearly as sociable as it once was. The chief reason for that is our good friend and neighbor, Cook, is no longer here. He died in 1992. Cook had thought his multiple sclerosis might protect him from AIDS—there were rumors and superstitions regarding MS and immunity—but it didn't. We visited him regularly in St. Vincent's Hospital around the corner. He wasn't our only friend who ended up there. Sometimes we had to decide which of two or even three people we would see on a given day. Cook's family was often in his room with him. His sister took his dog Fred home with her when he became sick. Nobody else holds court out here on the stoop the way that Cook and Fred once did.

Only a few of us old-timers remain. There's Sam upstairs with us on the fifth floor, and Bo on the first floor. Bill, the straight know-it-all cabdriver and lawyer, is still here, too, but a different version of him. I will tell his story in time. Our four apartments are the only ones still rent stabilized and we're protected. The rents are so high for everyone else, however, that new people come and go before we can get to know them. Even Jenny, a smart and pretty photographer from Sweden, stayed just long enough for us to want to know her better, and for her cute husband to fix a broken spring in our oven door.

In the window of the empty basement apartment to my right is a large white placard advertising condos for sale. It's a non-eviction plan, which means protected tenants can stay and continue to rent. We certainly can't afford to buy. We saw the offering package and learned our three-room five-floor walk-up is worth $650,000. Our landlord's decision to condomize could not have been more badly timed, however. The apartments went on sale a month before the real estate market crashed. He has not sold a single unit.

Cowley writes that Greenwich Village in 1924 was a mixed neighborhood of bohemian artists and Italian working-class families, with a few posh residences stranded here and there like islands of money. The working-class is gone now except for a handful of rent-stabilized holdouts, including an elderly couple who live on the top floor of the Rowley brownstone. The Italians poured in around 1900 and poured out again twenty years later, leaving behind cafes and bakeries and Catholic churches. The rich people who recently poured in are sure to pour out eventually, too, but it's hard to imagine they will leave behind anything of value, only swimming pools that will need to be filled in, and overpriced restaurants that will go out business. We are already seeing a lot of the latter.

Draper and I have lived in this building for thirty years now, longer than either of us have lived anywhere else. But other neighbors lived here longer.

Nina, of Tom and Nina, the parents of Sam the Baby, grew up in that same apartment with her parents and *three* siblings. When she and Tom had a second child, they moved to Westchester. She and I were talking about living space before they left and she confessed that the hardest part was that they had only one bathroom. "But how did you manage with six people when *you* were a child?" I asked. She looked surprise. "I don't know." Then I remembered I too grew up in a house with six people and only one bathroom. Did folks simply have bigger bladders in the old days?

Wendy, the little old lady with the German shepherd and the burning mattress, grew up in this building, too. Her father was an opera singer with the Met. She loved music herself. Draper put her in one of his movies, strolling down a street singing "Most Gentlemen Don't Like Love." Wendy claimed to be in her eighties but was actually ten years older. She became confused her last year here, wandering the building and knocking on doors. Draper opened our door one morning to find Wendy standing in the hall wearing only a sweater, naked from the waist down. "Hello, Shreeve," she said. "Uh, Wendy, you need to get back to your apartment and get dressed," said Draper, and he gently took her by the hand and led her downstairs. A niece eventually put Wendy in a nursing home. After she died, her ashes were scattered under the niece's rosebush.

Bill, too, has been here longer than we have. But we don't know how much longer he will remain.

When I last wrote about Bill, he was still married. His daughter Regina was ten and Bill had just finished law school. I frequently ran into him out front, coming home in a light blue seersucker suit with a briefcase in his hand. But then Peggy left him, taking Regina with her out to Queens. We never learned the details, but Bill could not have been an easy man to live with. Regina frequently stayed with her father on weekends and he helped her with her schoolwork and her applications to college. Bill often told me what Regina was reading and how smart she was. He was very proud of her.

Then Regina stopped coming to visit. Bill spoke less about his law work when I ran into him—until one afternoon I spotted him on the street behind the wheel of a taxi cab; he ducked so I wouldn't see him. Apparently his legal practice wasn't working out.

When Bill caught me reading on the front stoop, he would still ask to see my book, then share his own experience or memories about the author or topic. But his stories grew less coherent, his cheeks redder, his garrulity louder. "You know, when I grew up in the city, my mother wouldn't let us sit on the stoop. She said it was low-class. Ha!" I knew his talk was fueled by alcohol, and it was no longer entertaining or always friendly. He once testily asked what I'd done with the Victorian sheet music he'd loaned me. I'd never borrowed it, but I played along and said I'd see if I still had it, trusting him to forget the next time he saw me, which he did.

Sam was closer to Bill than we were—each had helped the other in times of crisis. He admitted Bill wasn't doing well, but he didn't know what to do. Finally I put in a call to a good friend, a psychiatrist who'd begun a new job with the city making house calls for psychiatric emergencies. He promptly got in touch with Adult Protective Services and they sent a team over. In a fictional tale, that would have been the happy ending, but it was only the beginning of a long, long, messy drama that is still going on. Bill's wife and daughter became involved in his life again. Police have visited more than once. One night a trio of surprisingly sweet street toughs brought Bill home after finding him drunk and badly hurt in a nearby park. Bill went into detox twice, and was in a clinic for six months. While he was away his wife and daughter went to work cleaning out his apartment to make it livable again. He had become a pack rat while living alone and his rooms were knee-high in debris—far worse than Wendy's apartment had been the night of the burning mattress. For weeks our hallway was full of fat garbage bags that were later taken down to the street. Since Bill returned from the clinic, he has been a ghost of himself, a pale old man with a wispy beard and baggy jeans who nods and says hi and little else. A caregiver comes by for a few hours each day. His wife says she has washed her hands of him, but we still run into her at the mailboxes.

Bo joins me on the stoop and asks what I'm reading. "Malcolm Cowley?" he says. "I don't know him. But the twenties? That would've been a fun decade to live here. *Before* the Crash."

Bo is a tall, lean, handsome man a few years older than me, a former sales rep for a fabric design house. He loves opera, movies and history. We regularly recommend titles to each other, mostly books about the Third Reich. It's a peculiar pre-dilection. Neither of us read it for horror or indignation, but out of a sad need to understand the world. Our need predates the invasion of Iraq, although my fascination with Germany deepened when I first understood that we too might be the bad guys.

"Nice weather," says Bo with a weary sigh. "Which means summer will soon be here and the Rowleys will be having pool parties directly outside my window."

"Hello, all," says Sam, bringing his feisty little terrier, Raqui (short for Raquel), down for a walk. Sam looks better than he did fifteen years ago, trimmer and healthier. He lowers his voice to ask me, "Could you call your psychiatrist friend? I think Bill might be drinking again but I don't want to confront him."

I explain there's little my friend can do now that Adult Protective Services is involved.

"Well, then, could you ask if he has any advice for how *I* might talk to him?"

It's curious that, of the five old-timers, the four gay guys do what we can to look after the straight guy.

But I don't find our building particularly sad. Stay in one place long enough and you follow a score of life stories to their end: all lives end in death. William Dean Howells famously complained that Americans want tragedies with happy endings. But you can follow any story past the tragedy to better times, if not for the dead then for the survivors.

Look at our city, for example: we survived September 11.

The World Trade Center was not visible from our apartment upstairs, but could be seen from the roof. Half a mile away, those stark twin posts, like two surveyor stakes, were never pretty, not even at sunrise when gold light sometimes glittered on the sides like fish scales. Yet the structure was reassuringly homely.

As everyone now remembers, the morning was lovely, clear and mild, with no humidity. Draper and I were home, sitting at opposite ends of our sofa, each reading a book—I was rereading *Buddenbrooks*—drinking coffee and enjoying the silence. We never turn on the TV in the morning. We heard a loud crash outside, like a car wreck on Seventh Avenue, followed by a collective gasp from a crowd. Wondering why so many people were on the street at that hour, I stuck head my head out the window. I saw nothing, so I raced out to the hall and upstairs to the roof. The twin towers stood downtown with a gaping hole in one and two long columns of smoke slowly blowing to the east. We had heard the second plane hit—we didn't hear the first. Tiny white specks like cigarette ash danced around the hole—we later learned these were thousands of sheets of paper blown into the sky. Time stood still.

When I ran back downstairs, I found Draper on the phone with his sister. The TV was on, locked on the very image that I had seen upstairs. Time continued to stand still. Draper's sister, watching TV in Kentucky, knew more about it than we did. But nobody knew very much that morning.

We made repeated trips between our apartment and the roof during the next hour. People stood on the rooftops all around, gesturing to each other and pointing at the towers as they spoke on cell phones. A young straight couple joined us on our roof, two drama students from California.

Then, at 9:59 A.M., the middle of the south tower swelled out a little, as if turning into smoke. The top section sank down into the smoke and it all dissolved in a black column of cloud. It was unreal. Not bad-movie-special-effects unreal but unthinkable unreal, unbelievable. The silence added to the unreality. Then the young woman beside us broke into loud sobs and it became real for us.

"We have just witnessed mass murder," said Draper.

Shortly afterward, I was downstairs on the phone talking with *my* sister when the second tower collapsed. I raced back up. But seeing it with the naked eye made it no more believable than seeing it on television.

The wilder reports on the news—that forty planes were unaccounted for, that the Mall in D.C. was on fire—were soon put to rest. It looked as if the worst was over. Then the newscaster said that hospitals needed blood. Draper and I hurried downstairs to go to St. Vincent's. The streets were full of people, but the city was strangely hushed, as if during a power failure. There was almost no traffic. Doctors and nurses stood at the entrance to the emergency room with wheelchairs and gurneys, waiting to tend survivors. Neighbors were already lining up to give blood. We followed the line around the block to Sixth Avenue, where we ran into my cousin, Maureen, and her lover, Meg. We all decided we could donate blood later, when they would still need it. But one of many sad facts about the event was that there were few survivors for the doctors to look after and the blood was never needed.

For the rest of the day, for the rest of the week, it felt like life would never be the same again. We waited for the next terrorist attack. We waited for full-scale war. Our friend Geoffrey, an abstract painter and teacher, had been a ten-year-old boy in London during the Blitz. He assured us this was bad but he had seen far worse.

The young couple who had stood on the roof with us moved out of New York by the end of the month. But everyone else remained. And the city slowly became itself again, with an enormous hole in it, both literal and cosmic. Our hour of chaos and death was eventually projected overseas in six years of chaos and death inflicted on a country that had had nothing to do with the attack. After watching three thousand innocent Americans die, I was sickened that we could turn around and kill a hundred thousand innocent Iraqis.

Bo and Sam and I are still chatting when the two twenty-something gay boys from the third floor burst out the door

and bound down the steps with their frisky new dog, an adolescent Weimaraner. The boys nod hi, but they're not as curious about us as their dog is about Raqui. We're invisible to
them, which I don't mind.

"Ah youth," says Sam irritably, watching them bounce
down the street. I don't even know their names.

Draper joins us. "Hello, boys," he says. "What a beautiful day."

"How's the film coming?" I ask.

"Oh, it's getting there."

Draper looks awfully good for a man in his fifties. He does
yoga twice a week and he eats wisely—more wisely than I do.
His hair is as grey as mine, but on him it looks good.

I stick Malcolm Cowley into our mailbox so I won't have to
carry the book. We wish Bo and Sam a pleasant evening and
head down toward the river.

Our block is quite grand now, with renovated stoops and
pretty shrubs and an expensive restaurant on the corner.
Next door to the restaurant, however, is the meeting room
of a local AA group, one of the toughest in the city we hear
from a friend who knows. Folks stand outside before and after
meetings, smoking cigarettes and drinking coffee, a wonderful assortment of gritty New Yorkers. We like having them at
our corner. It keeps our street real.

Because much of the street has become artificial. In the
next block is the brownstone used for the exterior of Carrie
Bradshaw's apartment in *Sex in the City*. She's supposed to
live on the Upper East Side, but Draper and I were watching
an episode on tape one night when I said, "Hey, I know that
corner in the background." We rewound and, sure enough,

it was the corner near the AA meeting. Walking past the brownstone a week later, we saw a woman out front watering her flowers. Draper struck a conversation. "Oh yes," she said. "They asked if they could use my stoop and front door for exteriors. They pay me something. I figure there's no harm in it."

A year later, tour groups began to arrive, busloads of young women with digital cameras. They lined up across the street to take each other's picture at Carrie's front door. Now and then a pissed-off neighbor told them that the real Carrie, Sarah Jessica Parker, lived just around the block. Why don't they go take their pictures on *her* stoop? The tourists only looked scornful, refusing to be taken for fools. Finally the woman in the brownstone strung a chain with a NO TRESPASSING sign across her steps, a chain and sign she has to replace every few months when they are stolen.

(Carrie Bradshaw never hung out on her stoop on TV, but one evening Draper and I passed Sarah Jessica Parker, her baby, and a couple of friends hanging out on *hers*.)

I tell Draper about my discovery in *Exile's Return*.

"Right next door? God, I wish there was a cheap pasta joint there now. Remember when there used to be cheap Italian places all over the neighborhood?"

Malcolm Cowley's Greenwich Village has disappeared behind facades of money and make-believe. It still exists in pockets, like the AA meeting or evenw our stoop, but is invisible to tourists. We are afraid it might die away completely. Draper and I frequently complain and sigh during our strolls. "Do you remember Sazarac House?" "Or The Front Porch?"

"Is that another nail salon?" "My god, are they opening a *sixth* Marc Jacobs store on Bleecker?" We probably sound like two old Russians pining for Moscow under the Tsar. Bo works in a nearby antique shop and says none of these new stores do much business except for Marc Jacobs and a bakery famous for the lines of suckers waiting to buy its mediocre cupcakes.

At the end of Perry Street stands a trio of glassy Richard Meier structures that Draper compares to giant ice trays. These luxury condos look awfully cold and dead, especially when half the floors are still empty. The crash that followed the housing boom has left us wondering what will happen to all these high-priced high-rises not even foreigners can afford to buy into. The West Village could become a futuristic ghost town.

But then we walk between the glass towers and come out to the river and our hearts lift a little. The Hudson is beautiful, wide and open—the new waterfront is actually a change for the better. Where old green warehouses used to sag into the river, or open piers stood crumbling in sunlight, there is a wide walkway with flowers and shrubs and young trees. Two new piers covered with grass reach out toward New Jersey. The bigger pier attracts swarms of sunbathers in warm weather, gay and straight, shingling the grass with a landscape of skin and swimsuits and underwear. They are replaced in the evening by gay black and Hispanic kids from uptown who come down here to a place where they feel safe to be themselves. They mix with the locals and everyone usually gets along.

The evening is beautiful. The blue sky overhead softly changes and the lights of Hoboken come on across the river. "And there's Czechoslovakia," says Draper, pointing out Ellis

Island in the distance with its steep roofs and baroque towers. The Statue of Liberty stands diminutively beside it.

At the end of the bigger pier is a pavilion with a twisty canvas roof like a piece of non-Euclidean geometry. Under the roof tonight, a tango club is meeting. We hear accordion music as we approach. There must be two dozen couples dancing, every kind imaginable: a short Asian man with a tall blond woman, a old woman with a young man, a young white woman with a young black woman. They slowly move clockwise around the center post where a large boom box plays. All around the dancers stand a friendly assortment of curious New Yorkers. Even the kids from uptown are silent, with one willowy boy standing off by himself, trying out a new dance step alone.

"It's like *Last Tango in Paris*," I say.

"*Last Tango in Manhattan*," says Draper.

We watch fascinated, admiring the way dancers improvise turns and gestures, stick a foot backward, pause, then dip and twirl a partner. We don't dare dance ourselves—these people are so good, so graceful—but it is a privilege to watch them perform this old-fashioned dance translated to a very new world. We lean against each other, shoulder to shoulder, and watch the circle of couples slowly come around one more time.

2009

ACKNOWLEDGMENTS

———~~~———

T HESE ESSAYS, ARTICLES and reviews
first appeared in the following maga-
zines and books: "Perry Street, Greenwich
Village," *Hometowns: Gay Men Write About
Where They Belong* (Dutton, 1992); "A Body in
Books," *James White Review* (Summer 2000);
"Slow Learners," *Boys Like Us: Gay Writers
Tell Their Coming Out Stories* (Avon, 1996);
"Little Green Buddies," *Christopher Street*
(May 1981); "Hearts of Stone: AIDS and the
Common Reader," *Lambda Book Report* (May
1992); "*Faggots* Revisited," *We Must Love One*

Another or Die (St. Martins, 1998); "Mapping the Territory," introduction to *Particular Voices* by Robert Giard (MIT Press, 1997); "George and Al," *Friends and Lovers: Gay Men Write about the Families They Create* (Dutton, 1995); "Homage to Mr. Jimmy," afterword to *Gods and Monsters* (reissue of *Father of Frankenstein*, Harper Perennial, 2005); "Glass Closet," *Lambda Book Report* (January 1999); "Can Straight Men Still Write?" *James White Review* (Winter 1999); "A Queer Monster," in a short version in *Meanjin* (v. ii, 2003) and full version in *James White Review* (Summer 2003); "Tattle Tale" published as "The Real David Brock," *Lambda Book Report* (June 2002); "A Sort of Friendship" published as "Delicate Monsters," *I Do, I Don't*, (Suspect Thoughts Press, 2004); "In Memory of Oscar Wilde (Bookstore)" was published in a shorter version in *The Guide* (March 2009).

"An Embarrassment of Books" and "Perry Street Redux" are published here for the first time.